Contents

Cover: The frivolous 'New Woman',
liberated from strait-laced corsets and
decorum. From the German fashion
magazine *Elegante Welt* (1913).
Front endpaper: A futuristic view (1896) of
'The Feminist Battalion at the Barricades'.
Rear endpaper: 'The day after tomorrow'
(1927): emancipated globetrotters in
bathing costumes, beside the new symbols
of freedom

Copyright © 1971: Trevor Lloyd
First published in 1971 by
BPC Unit 75
St Giles House 49 Poland St London W1
in the British Commonwealth and
American Heritage Press
551 Fifth Avenue New York NY 10017
in the United States of America
Library of Congress Card Catalogue
Number: 77-957 19
Made and printed in Great Britain by
Purnell and Sons Ltd Paulton Somerset

SUFFRAGETTES
INTERNATIONAL

The world-wide cam~
f~   ght·

COLLEGE OF HIGHER EDU
(Sion Hill)
LIBRARY

Trev

....

Library of the 20th Century
General Editor : John Roberts

Chapter 1
Beginnings

In England 'votes for women' meant suffragettes breaking glass and chaining themselves to railings. Events in England were only one part of a movement that was active all over the world, but although their approach was not typical of the long struggle, for a few years they held the centre of the stage.

Perhaps English women were more determined than any of the others, or English men resisted more unreasonably, or perhaps English society was so restrained and restricted that people welcomed the chance to let fly in a cause that they could take seriously. In any case, the militant suffragettes taught political agitators a good many lessons for the future — some of which are being put into practice at the present day.

Most of the women who wanted the vote were entirely conventional, except on this one issue. They were brought up as good strong-minded Victorian pillars of society in an age when Victorianism was not confined to England. Queen Victoria herself disapproved of women who wanted the vote and thought they deserved to be whipped, but in their determination and high-mindedness most of the women who wanted the vote had a lot in common with the Queen of England. Of course, if the Queen herself had been in favour of the vote, it might have made a considerable difference. She could never have announced her opinions publicly, but if people at the top of British society had been reminded of the rights of women by a woman whom they had to take seriously, the story might have been different, and much shorter.

Queen Victoria, and those who admired her, accepted a set of rules and conventions that severely limited the role of women in society and eventually provoked the feminist movement. Some of these conventions look more restricting than they were in fact: for instance, there were very strict rules about what could be written, especially in English-speaking countries. Victorian literature has a heavy air of sexual propriety about it and people today are surprised to find that the private lives of

Left: An early lampoon (1819) on women's fight for equality

5

the Victorians were much less restrained than their literature.

The convention that wives should be obedient to their husbands was obeyed some of the time: the husband was expected to be the head of the household, and often lived up to his role. But when the wife was the stronger personality, authority naturally drifted into her hands. This did not help women in the struggle for equality: it encouraged the anti-feminists to say that a skilful and intelligent woman could get her own way by exerting influence on men without any need to possess any legal rights.

But the convention that handicapped women most severely was the idea that a woman's place was in the home. This applied fairly exclusively to women of the upper and middle classes — poor people might have liked women to stay at home, but they could not afford it, except in the sense that a great many working-class women lived in other people's homes as servants.

Women had no place in the professions, except in the Catholic Church, where they were able to join religious orders. They could not become priests or clergymen, which excluded them from a much wider range of positions than it would at the present time. They could not become lawyers or doctors, and they had great difficulty in becoming merchants or traders because of legal restrictions on women's right to inherit or to own property.

'A woman's place is in the home' was a conservative slogan, which described the existing state of affairs and declared that it ought to continue. The right to vote was only one of a number of changes sought in the position of women. When the struggle began, around the middle of the 19th century, women claimed that they needed the vote in order to achieve the other changes. But by the time they got the vote most of the other changes for which they had been asking had already been made: women could go to universities, they could become doctors, they could get divorces if their marriages had collapsed catastrophically, and they could earn their own living.

18th-century beginnings

The upheaval in ideas which accompanied the French Revolution led to some questioning of women's position in society. Jean-Jacques Rousseau, the 18th-century French philosopher, wrote that man was born free, but he showed in his writing (and in the way he treated his wife) 10 ▷

Far right: The submissive sex — woman as drudge (top) and plaything (bottom). Right: Women's clubs fulminated against the suffocating female role. Next page: 'The salon in the Rue des Moulins', Toulouse-Lautrec's vision of a Paris brothel

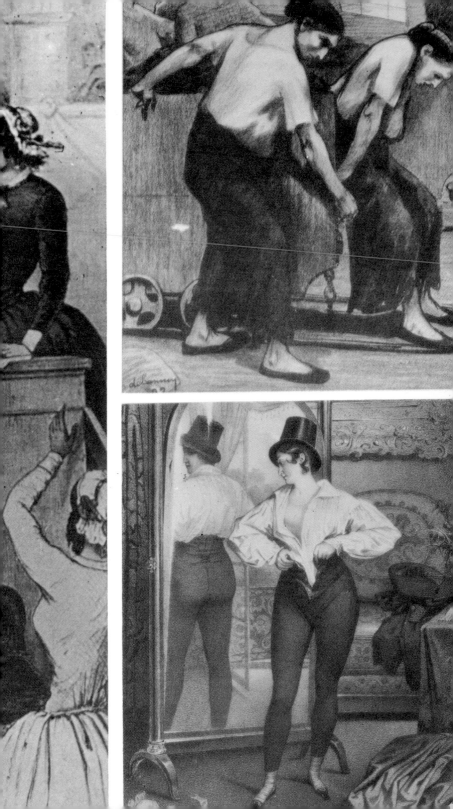

that this was not meant to apply to women. But discussion about the rights of men led on logically to Mary Wollstonecraft's *Vindication of the Rights of Women* in 1792. It did not have much effect, and Horace Walpole called her 'a hyena in petticoats' for her pains, but it was a beginning.

Mary Wollstonecraft paid little attention to the right to vote and did not consider it very important. Few men had the right to vote in 18th-century England, and women were not always without political influence: in the famous 1784 election in Westminster the Duchess of Devonshire had canvassed for Charles James Fox, and had kissed some electors to win their votes. It was not the same as having votes of their own, but women showed no signs of wanting to vote.

In France, Mme Roland played a more serious role in politics during the Revolution. Her salon became the intellectual centre of the Girondin party and she was generally believed to guide her husband's policy while he was Minister of the Interior. It did her no good: she was guillotined by the Jacobins and is now remembered mainly for her comment: 'Liberty, what crimes are committed in your name!' But Mme Roland was obliged to work indirectly: women did not get the vote during the Revolution. Olympe de Gouges petitioned the Constituent Assembly and the Convention for women's rights. The revolutionaries took her seriously and—perhaps because they reckoned that women would oppose the anticlerical aspects of the Revolution—guillotined her too.

In the twenty years between the end of the bloodthirsty period of the French Revolution and the fall of Napoleon in 1815, the most conspicuous political woman in Europe was Mme de Staël. It was not always easy to take her seriously; her love-affairs were conducted at the top of her voice and, although the times were such that few people found them shocking, a great many found them ridiculous. All the same, her constant pressure for freedom of speech and freedom of the press upset Napoleon so much that he hounded her mercilessly. In return she intrigued against him incessantly and her persistence was acknowledged (though of course exaggerated) in the remark that there were three great powers against Napoleon: England, Russia, and Mme de Staël.

This was not a matter of boudoir intrigue; her love-affairs seldom had much to do with her political activity. She conducted a salon which, while not avowedly anti-Napoleon, definitely favoured free speech. She wrote novels, political theory, and literary criticism that attempted to combine the qualities of 18th-century reasonableness with the enthusiasm of the new romantics. For all her political zeal, however, she seems to have

shown no interest in votes for women. Freedom of speech rather than freedom to vote was always her main concern.

The question remained dormant. William Thompson's *Appeal of One Half the Human Race against the Pretensions of the Other Half,* which came out in 1825, was perhaps the first full-fledged statement of the case for giving women the vote but it attracted very little attention. Neither men nor women in England in the first half of the 19th century had any political cause which made women want to take part in politics.

American suffragettes

Things were different in the United States. Abolition of slavery attracted women, who were eager to play an active part in the campaign. Emancipation for women and emancipation for slaves seemed to have something in common: Oberlin College, for instance, was the first college to take women, and it also took Negro students. But at times the presence of women divided the abolitionists; when women were chosen as delegates from the United States to an anti-slavery conference in London, they were not admitted and were sent upstairs to the gallery instead. William Lloyd Garrison, one of the great abolitionist leaders, arrived a little later and insisted on joining the women in the gallery as a protest. But while determined abolitionists like Garrison were ready for women to be active in the movement, the more sedate reformers continued to feel that women should not be seen too much and should not be heard at all.

Reform movements such as the anti-slavery movement were made up of the sort of middle-class people who would have found the Duchess of Devonshire's electoral activity particularly shocking—Jane Austen, who kept her novel-writing a secret from her relations, was much closer to their ideal of what a lady should be. And yet ladies did do a good deal of the more boring work for reform organisations—like raising funds by holding bazaars.

During the 1840s American women grew more and more dissatisfied with the way the various reform organisations treated them. After a temperance organisation had spent almost the whole of a three-day conference arguing whether they should let a woman member give a speech or not, a women's rights meeting was held in July 1848 at Seneca Falls in New York State. Even at

Top: Mme de Staël **(left)** and Mme de Pompadour, Louis XV's mistress **(right)**: European powers in their own right, who combined strong minds with ease of access to influential bedrooms. **Middle:** An 18th-century French salon, centre of female power. **Bottom:** Early cartoon (1819) of female reformers

11

this meeting women's right to vote was asserted less confidently than the right to own property, to obtain a divorce, and to enter the professions.

One inhabitant of Seneca Falls was determined to take practical steps to increase women's freedom. Shortly after the meeting Amelia Jenks Bloomer launched a new costume – a calf-length dress over ankle-length pantaloons – which made it distinctly easier for women to walk about and do their work. But the new fashion was regarded as ridiculous and indecent, and during the 1850s women took to ever-wider and less convenient styles of crinolines. Another American, Dr Mary Walker, tried to lead a movement for more practical clothes in the 1860s but nothing came of it. In England Lady Harberton launched the Rational Dress Association in 1880. This was a little more successful because of the spreading enthusiasm for tennis and cycling in the next couple of decades, but on the whole 19th-century women remained determined to dress in a way that severely limited their freedom.

American women went on working for the abolition of slavery, for temperance, and for other good causes, but they became more and more convinced that the causes they supported would advance more quickly if they had the vote. In the 1860s the Civil War raised high hopes. As in all subsequent wars, women took on some of the work of men while the fighting was going on. They showed that they could make use of the opportunity, and they hoped that men would be grateful after the war.

Wyoming presages the future

But when the war was over the politicians of the victorious North decided to introduce complete emancipation for Negroes, including the vote. Women had to wait even though President Johnson would have preferred votes for women to come first. At first they thought it would be a matter of one or two sessions of Congress, but gradually they realised that men's reforming zeal could die down quite quickly in the face of opposition. In the far west something was gained: when the Territory of Wyoming was created in 1869, women were given the vote on a basis of equality, and the inhabitants stuck to their decision despite attempts to push them into abandoning their eccentric ideals.

Men did not mind so much if women were allowed to vote in local elections – they had been given the right to vote in municipal elections in Sweden in 1862 – but voting for the central government was another matter. In any case, Wyoming was not a state – it was only a municipal council ruling several million empty miles.

'Mrs Satan' for President

After the Civil War the fervour of reform in the United States burnt fairly low for some years to come, but a women's suffrage movement had been established in 1869 and it kept the fight alive. It very soon split, as such movements will do, into an activist and a respectable section. The bone of contention was a Mrs Woodhull; she advocated free love and clearly practised it, she ran a stockbroker's office (helped by the friendship of the railroad magnate 'Commodore' Vanderbilt) at a time when Wall Street was much rougher than it is now, and she managed through her connections in Congress to present the women's case to a congressional committee at Washington for the first time.

She was an ideal leader if women were to get the vote in a single determined rush, but a liability if it came down to a long slow round of lobbying and arguing and proving that women would not do anything rash or unconventional if they had the vote. The activists in the National Woman Suffrage Association naturally supported Victoria Woodhull, and the respectable American Woman Suffrage Association equally naturally disapproved of her. It was a struggle between New York, her home base, where her behaviour was not completely unacceptable, and the other areas where the Suffrage Associations were strong, which tended to agree when she was nicknamed Mrs Satan. Victoria Woodhull ran for President in 1872 (there was nothing to stop her being a candidate), took up spiritualism, and died fifty years later as the wife of an English banker—her sister Tennessee, who had supported her in all her activities, did even better, and died Lady Cook. Victoria Woodhull's career left the American suffrage societies divided for twenty years, though probably no organisation could have made progress during the Gilded Age and the loss of interest in reform that followed the Civil War and Reconstruction.

Women's suffrage became an issue, though with much less preparation, in Great Britain in the 1860s. The philosopher John Stuart Mill had been elected to Parliament in 1865, and when the second Reform Bill was being debated in 1867 he moved an amendment to give votes to women. It was defeated, 194 to 73, but the minority was large enough to surprise and encourage its supporters. For the rest of the century backbenchers moved Private Members' Bills in most sessions of Parliament; this was good publicity for votes for women, but no government took any interest in the suggestion, so opponents of the change could always stop it by talking the Bills out and never letting them come to a vote.

Left: An idealistic French allegory of universal suffrage, 1848

Mill was defeated in the 1868 general election, and the next year he published his book *On the Subjection of Women*. He pointed out a great many ways in which women's legal position was inferior to that of men, and argued that the best way to change this was to give women the vote. In fact, the position of women was already changing without the help of the vote. Mill pointed out that married women were not allowed by the law to have any property of their own—extravagant husbands could spend all their own money and could then go on to waste their wives' money as well. But in a matter of a dozen years this abuse had been put right, and wives could keep their own money, while the question of votes passed more or less out of sight.

In France Léon Richier published his book *The Rights of Women* in 1869. The next year, when the Second Empire fell and was replaced by a republic, the prospects for women might appear to have improved under a constitution which was based on universal suffrage. Mme Barbarousse claimed the right to vote on the grounds that *tout français* had been enfranchised; in 1885 the courts declared that, at least so far as the franchise went, 'Frenchmen' did not embrace 'French women'. But here again the tendency to change, unaffected by the vote, could be seen. The *Code Napoléon,* produced at the beginning of the century, had laid down strict rules that placed women in an inferior position: it was accepted as law in France throughout the changes of constitution during the 19th century, and it had a considerable effect in defining the position of women to their disadvantage in a number of other countries as well. Yet it was in the 1880s, when women were being told that the law could not be interpreted in a way that gave them the vote, that the attitude of the *Code Napoléon* was relaxed and divorce was permitted under certain circumstances.

The main reason for the improvement in women's position, in France and elsewhere, was that women could get better jobs than before. Country women had always worked in the fields before they married—after marriage they went on working in the fields, and they withered under the strain of fieldwork combined with running the house. If they did not get married, they could make a little money spinning—hence the word 'spinsters'. Industrialisation and the move to the towns opened up a great many new jobs for men, but not so many for women at first. Spinning and weaving were still the women's jobs; the lucky ones got jobs in the hot, damp

cotton factories, and the less fortunate had to work at home, trying to accept a low enough wage to compete with machinery. Thomas Hood's *The Song of the Shirt,* about an underpaid seamstress, did not stray from the facts, as the British House of Commons found when it investigated conditions in the 'sweated' trades — sewing or making matchboxes or stitching clothes together in the early years of this century.

The 'life of shame'
Trapped in this position of few jobs and low wages, women inevitably took to prostitution. According to middle-class legend, any woman who took to the streets was branded for ever. This was by no means always the case; obviously it was a dangerous job, with rough clients and a much larger chance of venereal disease than at the present day, but all the evidence suggests that there was an astonishingly large number of prostitutes in large cities and that they very often married and settled down when their working days were over.

In the 1890s Bernard Shaw's play *Mrs Warren's Profession* caused a great deal of fuss by suggesting that a girl from the working class was much better off as a prostitute than at work in a white-lead factory where she was likely to die a slow and painful death from phosphorus poisoning. The play was banned in London by the Lord Chamberlain, though in New York the examining magistrate said that it was fit to perform.

The play also had a message of hope because Mrs Warren's daughter could hope for a respectable and more permanent job as an actuary. This was rather an optimistic ending; the young heroine of the play had just come top of the mathematics examination at Cambridge University (a topical point, for Phillippa Fawcett, daughter of the great suffragist leader Millicent Fawcett, managed this in 1890), and so she was eminently employable. Her position, with such rare qualifications, was as unusual as those of the girls at the top of her mother's profession who rose to international celebrity, like Cora Pearl, a leading figure in the demi-monde of Napoleon III, or Mrs Langtry, who was the friend of respectable men like Gladstone although it was quite clear that she was being financially supported by her lover, the Prince of Wales (later Edward VII).

An ordinary middle-class girl would not be able to start work as an actuary, just as she would have been very ill-advised to imagine that she could preserve her social standing as well as Mrs Langtry, if she plunged into

Left: 19th-century male attitudes to woman: the slave of her domineering husband (top), and the tender innocent (bottom)

what respectable Victorians would call a 'life of shame'. The question still remained: how could the middle-class girl earn a living? A few very brilliant women supported themselves as authors and journalists: Harriet Martineau's success as a journalist in England in the mid-19th century showed that it could be done. But when a great writer like Charlotte Brontë had to support herself, with some difficulty, as a teacher, the prospects for women were not good.

'Nightingale nurses'

Florence Nightingale won a unique position during the Crimean War; she organised hospitals and saved the British army from the worst results of its bad organisation and failure to make provision for the cruel winter of 1854-55. And for the next forty years she used the great prestige gained in the Crimea as an adviser on matters of government medical policy. She made nursing into a respectable profession that women could join without being taken for the drunken Mrs Gamp of Dickens's novel. She also made it scientific. At a time when doctors had very few drugs and anaesthetics, nursing was even more important for the patient's survival than at the present day. 'Nightingale nurses', instructed according to her principles, steadily raised hospital standards in England and in other countries.

These nurses were still not well-paid, partly because people thought of nursing as a way of life for devoted women with private means like Florence Nightingale herself, and partly because of the situation on the continent of Europe, where orders of nuns like the *soeurs de charité* worked as nurses under vows of poverty. In the middle of the 19th century they had been providing much more conscientious service than was available in most Protestant countries.

But in spite of Florence Nightingale's efforts to raise nursing standards, by the end of the century the nursing orders had heavily diluted their numbers with lay helpers who were not much better than the pre-Nightingale nurses had been. Reform was inevitable. At the beginning of the 20th century, Anna Hamilton published a thesis on nursing that encouraged the doctors in France to take action: they set up schools of nursing first at Bordeaux and then in several other cities including Paris. Municipal councils co-operated, partly out of a desire for better nursing and partly as a move in the campaign against the religious orders in the aftermath of the Dreyfus Case. The nursing orders were driven out of

Right: *'Women for sale' — a French view of the Englishman's market-place attitude to marriage in the early 19th century*

18

their positions. Similar developments took place in Belgium: after a quarrel with a nursing order, the anticlerical Dr Depage decided to launch a training scheme for nurses along Nightingale lines. An English nurse was needed to be the first director, and in 1907 the job was given to Edith Cavell.

But these changes did not much alter the economic situation. When Ibsen wrote *The Doll's House* in 1873, the play ended with Nora, a middle-class housewife, walking out of her husband's house and slamming the door. A great lady who ran a large household was doing a full-time administrative job, and a working-class housewife looking after home and family had more than enough to do. But in middle-class homes it was expected that the work would be done by servants, and the housewife had no purpose in life except to be admired and played with by her husband. But when Nora slammed the door, what was she to do next? Earning a living was probably even harder for a respectable woman on the continent of Europe than in England: George Sand (who often wore men's clothes as well as taking a man's name) gained fame through her novels and notoriety by her affair with Chopin; in the 1860s Rosa Bonheur won some position as a painter; and a little later Sarah Bernhardt attained universal renown as an actress. But women like these were exceptional and nobody would call them respectable or consider them any encouragement for giving women the vote.

The seed-bed of the suffragist movement was the increase in the number of respectable middle-class jobs open to women in the second half of the 19th century. In the United States, Elizabeth Blackwell was able to open up the way to becoming a doctor and later played a considerable role in medical organisation during the Civil War. But in England in the 1850s there was bitter resistance to pioneer women like Elizabeth Garrett Anderson and Sophia Jex-Blake. Hospitals and colleges for medical education changed their rules of admission for the specific purpose of keeping women out and, when the legal barriers had been overcome, the medical students tried to exclude the women by jostling and insulting and pelting them. The behaviour of the Edinburgh students was just like that of white people in the American South anxious to prevent integration of their schools a hundred years later, and it was strongly suspected that the professors encouraged this display of student disorder. But admission to the medical profession was not always a sign of how public opinion would react to votes for

Top right: A French satire on women in the civil service (1869). Bottom right: Women type-setters. Right: Seamstresses

20

women: in 1870—by which time there were already 575 women doctors in the United States—both France and Sweden allowed women to become doctors, though public opinion was much less tolerant of women's emancipation in France than in Sweden.

Women had been employed as teachers for many years, and the expansion of education (combined with the reduction in the size of classes) in the 19th century increased the number of jobs. But a high standard of respectability was always expected of school-teachers: school boards preferred to employ unmarried women only, and even in the most Protestant of countries women teachers were expected to behave like members of a strict religious order. Teachers were expected to behave as though they had taken vows of chastity, obedience, and poverty—as was shown by the teacher training college in the 1880s which refused to install baths on the grounds that it would not be a good idea to give teachers a taste for luxury which they would never again be able to afford. School-teachers were an advance-guard of women who could earn their own living, but they were not able to do much to strengthen the suffragettes.

The typist revolution

The decisive shift in the economic position of women came with the expansion and simplification of office work. In the middle of the 19th century the office clerk possessed qualities which were in short supply—literacy and honesty with money. By the end of the century these qualities, though still necessary, were no longer in short supply. There seemed to be an endless stream of young girls prepared to be book-keepers or 'typewriters', the late 19th-century word for typists. Of course many of these girls could now earn their living if the need arose; they did not have to concentrate on finding a husband, and if they failed to do so they did not have to look forward to becoming pitied dependants of their families.

As the years have gone by, this stream of girls going into office work has broadened into a flood. Today office work has replaced domestic service as the dominant occupation among women in Europe and North America. But this change had not taken place by the time of the great struggle for the vote: domestic servants were still relatively easy to find, and young ladies who worked in offices—usually middle-class pioneers—were still a novelty, though a novelty which was rapidly becoming a necessity. For some decades the telephone system was worked manually by girls who plugged lines into sockets to put calls through; if telephone calls were still to be put through in this way today, the whole female population of the United States would be at work putting plugs

into sockets. But the telephone girl was in her time one sign that women were gaining greater economic freedom.

Ladies complaining about the servant problem would say that the young girls had gone off to work in factories. This does not seem very likely. Girls who were servants in the better sort of family (these complaints about the shortage of servants always came from ladies who explained how attractive their homes were) went into the simpler type of office work rather than into factories. But the servant problem had not really reached a crisis before 1914, and the girl in the office was still the middle-class pioneer rather than the ordinary girl who takes it for granted that she can dive into the typing pool even if she cannot become anything more interesting.

At the same time as office jobs became easier to find, and servants became harder to keep, housekeeping became simpler. Shopping had been in the past an immensely time-consuming business in which customers went out and bargained with shopkeepers about each item on sale. The Quakers in England and America are said to have been among the first shopkeepers to stop bargaining and put a price-ticket on their goods below which they refused to go.

The Quakers' fixed price was not only more truthful but it was also more convenient for shoppers, who could get what they wanted quickly. Bargaining went on, even in prosperous countries, among the very poor and the very rich, buying in small quantities or buying very special products. But for most things bargaining became difficult with the growth of large manufacturing or food-processing chains. When sugar was put into neatly-wrapped packets—by the Tate family (the Lyle family was in golden syrup)—something closer to a standard price per packet was charged than in the days when the grocer scooped it out of a barrel and weighed it himself. And the packaged food was less likely to be adulterated; the local grocer had a nasty habit of putting a little sand into his sugar barrel, but the large food processors were more careful of their reputations. Food in tin-cans had appeared by the end of the 19th century and made life easier, though it was soon regarded as a sign of bad housekeeping.

Changes in home furnishing also saved time. Victorian furniture was heavy and hard to move, and the fashion for quantities of decorations, ornaments, and knick-knacks involved an immense amount of dusting. And for most of the century the dusting was made all the

Left: Fashion sheds its weight. **Top:** *'The Bum Shop' by Row-landson (c. 1780).* **Middle:** *'Bloomerism' (c. 1850).* **Bottom:** *The revelation of the ankle (c. 1914) and the knee (c. 1925)*

grimier because rooms were lit by candles or by a sooty sort of gas-lamp. In the 1880s the gas-mantle reduced the sootiness of this sort of lamp, and electricity provided the first completely clean form of illumination. The general clutter of the Victorian home began to disappear in the face of the attitude expressed in William Morris's slogan 'Have nothing in your home that you do not know to be useful or believe to be beautiful'. As the flood-tide of knick-knacks receded, women acquired more freedom simply because they had more time. Other little inventions helped: chopping up soap bars into soapflakes made washing easier, and so did the early washing-machines which took women away from the washing-tub and the mangle. The vacuum-cleaner came a bit later, but there is a moving passage in Arnold Bennett about the Ewbank floor-sweeper, which at the end of the century was the last word in modernity, at least in the homes of Great Britain's industrial areas.

These changes made it easier for middle-class women to earn their own living because they had more time, and also meant that women who did not have to earn their own living could spend much less time looking after the house. The liberation of young girls from the need to find a husband as soon as possible was one of the foundations of the movement to get the vote; their leaders were married or respectably widowed women with plenty of time for the tasks of organisation. It was said that the suffragettes were women who had failed to find husbands or, as Marie Corelli, a fashionable novelist who was never sorry to find a way to remind people of her charms, put it in 1907, 'One never sees any pretty women among those who clamour for their rights.'

Opponents of giving votes to women said that clever and attractive women could persuade men to see things their way, and thus had political power without needing a vote. Why it was only the attractive women who deserved to have political power was never explained, but the argument was often heard that women who went out to ask for their rights were in some way dissatisfied with home life or their failure to find a husband and set up a home. The leaders of the movement must, in fact, have had remarkably happy homes: without the loyal support of their families they could never have got their work accomplished.

Left: *Revolution in the home: 1874 'washing, wringing, and mangling machine'* **(top left)**; *1873 cooker* **(top right)**; *1909 vacuum cleaner* **(bottom left)**; *sewing machine* **(bottom right)**

25

Chapter 2
Good Causes

Several political issues not directly concerned with the right to vote were fought in the last decades of the century. Problems like licensed prostitution were in some ways even more difficult than the fight for the vote. In the 1860s the British House of Commons had passed the Contagious Diseases Acts which said that in towns where troops were billeted, women suspected of being prostitutes could be compulsorily examined for venereal disease – and in the days before Wassermann tests examination was an unpleasant process. Compulsory examination upon suspicion inevitably led to trouble when the examiners mistakenly picked on respectable women, but nobody expected the respectable women to do anything about it. But they had in Josephine Butler a remarkably talented leader: they put forward candidates at by-elections, asked questions at general elections and lobbied MPs while Parliament was sitting. This was one of the first pressure-groups run mainly by women to be successful; after about fifteen years of struggle and argument the Acts were repealed.

The compulsory examinations of respectable women provided the campaign with a certain amount of its propaganda, but the deeper criticism of the Acts was that they treated women as though they were just instruments for men's pleasure, who ought to be supervised for the convenience of the men. The Acts had been seen as a considerable interference with liberty in England; in countries like France and Italy, where the trade was already neatly supervised and was run by brothels which were to a greater or lesser extent state-approved, women were being much more systematically treated as instruments of pleasure. Josephine Butler went on from her success with the British House of Commons to help direct European agitation against the system of brothels. This was a much longer task, but when the League of Nations was set up after the First World War its social agencies ac-

Left: The bicycle was a harbinger and symbol of emancipated woman. Decorative cycling motifs from an Italian magazine

cepted the need to fight the 'white slave trade' which kid-
napped girls and forced them to work as prostitutes by
keeping them locked up in brothels. This part of its
work met with some success; and after the Second World
War licensed and approved brothels were closed down in
France and Italy. Prostitution still goes on, but at least
it is to a large extent a trade that girls have chosen for
themselves and can leave when they want to.

In the United States brothels existed mainly as a convenient way of rewarding the police for not enforcing
laws against prostitution. As such they were not a direct
interference with girls' freedom in the same way as
French and Italian brothels were and so were less objec-
tionable to reformers of Mrs Butler's views.

The Demon Drink
The campaign for the prohibition of alcoholic drink in the
United States was on a far larger scale than anything
Mrs Butler dreamed of, but at some points it was comparable. Women played a considerable role in the struggle; the Women's Christian Temperance Union was always prominent in local referendums and in elections—it
was dry policy to support any party, Republican, Demo-
crat, or Populist, which was ready to give convincing
dry pledges. And at the level of direct action, Carrie
Nation (a woman whose religious zeal had been a little
too much for her balance of mind) used to go round with
her axe, march into saloons, and chop up the bar and
break the glassware, bottles, and all.

The campaign against the Contagious Diseases Acts in
England was kept separate from the movement to get the
vote, in case it made votes for women seem an unrespec-
table cause; in the United States the leaders of the campaign for the vote tried not to become associated with the
Prohibition agitation, but their prudent efforts were in
vain. Prohibition would appeal to women if it appealed
to anyone; the pleasures of getting drunk were usually
reserved for men (though not always), and their wives
then had to cope with a violent husband who had poured
too much of the housekeeping money down his throat.
The drunkard's wife was in a pitiable situation, and the
propaganda of the Prohibitionists lost no opportunity to
remind everyone about it. And so female supporters of
prohibition quite naturally said that women ought to be
given the vote so that they could vote against the 'demon
drink'. Women who wanted the vote often co-operated
with this approach and claimed that drunkenness was
one of the many evils that would be reduced once women
had the vote.

But whatever the real relationship between heavy
drinking and votes for women, the liquor interests,

brewers, distillers, publicans, and saloon-owners, and the ordinary man who liked a drink all came to believe that 'votes for women' meant Prohibition for men. And as a result any opponent of Prohibition was a potential opponent of votes for women. The supporters of votes for women may have overestimated the importance of the liquor interest, and attributed to its hostility failures that were really due to the fact that a great many men were quite satisfied with things as they were, and did not see why votes for women would be any improvement. All the same, the liquor trade did provide some organisation for the opponents of enfranchisement.

The trapped wife

For whatever reason, the 1870s and 1880s were not a period of progress for women on the issue of the suffrage, though other changes went forward, or at least became established as causes which could expect success. The attack on the existing structure of marriage was beginning. *The Doll's House* had attacked the falsity of a marriage which was, by the standards of the time, peaceful and happy, but many marriages were much less successful, and they were very hard to dissolve. In the United States the rules varied from state to state but tended not to be accommodating; in England adultery by the wife was grounds for divorce but adultery by the husband would serve only if it was accompanied by cruelty; in almost all of Europe divorce was unthinkable though it might be legal. In the upper classes these things could be managed, though at the cost of considerable loss of social standing; in the urban working class there was frequently no marriage ceremony, and so no problem of divorce. In the middle class the indissolubility of marriage was more of a burden, and the reaction against it was sometimes extreme.

In Manchester in the late 1870s the youthful and impetuous Emmeline Goulden put it to Dr Richard Pankhurst that marriage was so unsatisfactory that they should form a 'free union'; Dr Pankhurst was a scrupulous man, and he pointed out to her that the laws and the economic conditions made free love as dangerous as marriage for a woman. They duly got married, and until his death twenty years later they carried on the work of agitation for a great many radical causes without attracting much attention.

The great American dancer, Isadora Duncan, was even

Left: 'Le style c'est la femme' — a French cartoon on fashion. Left from top: Baby-doll for brothel madame, the instant undress, the artistic, the chic. Right: The fetishistic, the homemade replica, the lure of beauty-spots, the small dressmaker

younger when she decided 'I would live to fight against marriage and for the emancipation of women' – according to her autobiography she was twelve years old, and the child of an unhappy marriage. She lived up to her programme, though eventually she decided that the system of marriage accompanied by divorce on demand by either party which had been established in Russia for the first few years after the Revolution was satisfactory. But before this she had shown that what she considered the important aspect of emancipation was the right of a woman to have children without having a husband. This, of course, was an extreme attitude but more moderate versions of the same idea were beginning to be heard fairly widely.

Public opinion was not prepared to accept this, but many people admitted that marriage could be a trap for women which deprived them of their freedom and left them at the mercy of a man whom they might have married without sufficient thought – of course, a marriage might be unsatisfactory for the husband, but in the last resort he could always abandon his home and desert his wife, a drastic solution that was virtually out of the question for her unless she had a job or a private income to fall back on.

Easier divorce and early birth control

In the United States, from about 1890 onwards, states altered their divorce laws in a way that made it easier to end marriages. This was not caused by votes for women; the changes in divorce law usually came before women had been given the right to vote. The increasing influence of women had some effect: women took an active interest in politics, and helped with party organisation, so that men might be concerned to conciliate women in politics even before they got the vote, but this indirect pressure was not likely to be decisive by itself. In fact, the men also wanted easier divorce laws.

Easier divorce did increase women's freedom and so did birth control. A certain amount had been known about birth control techniques for centuries, but the idea that the knowledge might be spread more widely as a way of fighting poverty and freeing women from bondage to child-bearing was a 19th-century development.

People had believed that if the poor had a little more money they would only spend it on having larger families. John Stuart Mill seems to have been among the first to see that this perpetuation of poverty could be avoided if

*Right: The first telephonists. **Top right:** Man's 'dissipation' provokes protest in an Arizona billiard-room. **Bottom right:** Caricature showing how the piano is taught at a girls' school*

the poor learnt something about birth control, which did not help his reputation. (Gladstone withdrew from a committee for a memorial to Mill when he learnt about this aspect of his work.) In the 1870s there were limited campaigns in England to provide advice and information; Charles Bradlaugh and Mrs Annie Besant were tried and convicted for circulating obscene literature, though the judge made it clear that he regarded the verdict as unjustified.

Giving advice and information in the United States was even harder—there was something very like a crusade to stop it. Anthony Comstock, who made a lifelong career out of seeking out all sorts of obscene literature and other manifestations of vice, persuaded state legislatures to pass new laws to prevent the sale of contraceptives and the spread of information, making it very hard for reformers to help the poor who went on having large families, many of whom died very young (in some cases helped on their way by their parents, who could not face the prospect of another mouth to feed).

Bradlaugh and Mrs Besant would have been regarded as disreputable even if they had had nothing to do with birth control; they were atheist lecturers and Bradlaugh was a declared republican—the pair of them stood in an old radical tradition which believed that Church and Crown were the enemies of the people, and that the way to help the people was to tell them what the world was really like.

Mrs Besant moved on from birth control to socialism. By the 1880s she was one of the best orators in England; in 1888 she organised and inspired a strike of the London match girls, and when the newly-founded Fabian Society published its *Fabian Essays in Socialism* in 1889, she was the only contributor who was already well known. If she had remained in English politics she would almost certainly have become a leader in the struggle for votes for women, and would have been a rare example of an unhappily married woman in the movement—she had been married to a clergyman, and had only become prominent after leaving him. But she gave up socialism for theosophy and, apart from a brief moment in the First World War when she helped persuade the Indian Congress Party to take a more militant line in the struggle for independence, she left the political scene for ever.

Her influence may have lingered on in another odd way; in 1907 Bernard Shaw wrote a play, *Getting Married*, **36** ▷

Right: *The girl of genteel background was carefully protected from the kind of harsh reality her working-class counterpart —such as this young girl operating complex machinery in a South Carolina cottonmill, c. 1900—was continually exposed to*

The New Woman

In 1852 Florence Nightingale had inveighed against the system of stifling gentility that oppressed all members of her class and sex: 'Give us back our suffering, suffering rather than indifferentism . . . for out of suffering may come the cure. Better have pain than paralysis.' The new spirit born of the struggle for equality manifested itself in a variety of fashionable or forward-looking freedoms: in the new sport of bicycling, for instance **(bottom right:** 'the Championess'), which baffled so many chaperones; in the scramble for tobacco **(top right);** and in the founding of women's university colleges **(below:** Bryn Mawr College, USA). When G.K. Chesterton wrote, 'Twenty million young women rose to their feet with the cry, "We will not be dictated to", and proceeded to become stenographers,' he was, as usual, not being wholly fair. Even an office job was an advance on the times when all serious activities were left to the men and woman's role was to be passive and stay-at-home

THE GREAT SMOKE QUESTION.
The Ladies (bless 'em) take it up.

in which the characters discuss the disadvantages of marriage, and wonder whether it might not be better for men and women to set up relationships by individually devised contracts. This was a bright idea, but Shaw did not really pursue it consistently, and he let the opponents of contract win the argument too easily. Perhaps the reason was that Shaw had already had to face the issue because in her Fabian days Annie Besant had been closely enough attached to him to suggest that they should enter into a contract (she was, of course, still married). When Shaw heard the terms she proposed he said it would take away even more of his freedom than marriage. He was probably exaggerating – any relationship with a personality as strong as Annie Besant would soon have restricted his freedom just as much.

New opportunities

The 'new woman' of the 1890s, who was just beginning to go to Bernard Shaw's plays, was the recruiting material that the suffrage movement needed. She played the new game of lawn tennis, and she benefited from the decline in fashion of billiards, an all-male game. She bicycled, and had a chance to make unexpected acquaintances – it was relatively easy to chaperone a girl at a dance but hard to provide a chaperone for a lady-cyclist, unless it was another relatively emancipated lady-cyclist.

If she was more serious-minded, it was easier for her to take an interest in social reform. By the end of the century Jane Addams had established Hull House as a centre for social work in Chicago which became a school for training social reformers (among them Mackenzie King, later Prime Minister of Canada for over twenty years). In England Miss Beatrice Potter found no real difficulties in her way when she wanted to find out about the problems of poverty in the East End of London – she disguised herself as a poor woman looking for work making cheap shirts, but it soon became so clear that her talent was for organisation rather than sewing that she was invited to marry the manager's son and settle down to run the business. Despite her excursions into the slums she continued to move in the best society. After she had married Sidney Webb, another early Fabian, they used her social position to get in touch with political leaders whom they then lobbied on behalf of their various crusades for social reform.

Early in her career of social investigation and research Beatrice Potter had been so far from feeling handicapped by her position as a woman that she signed a petition drawn up by Mrs Humphrey Ward the novelist, deploring the agitation for giving women the vote. Later on she decided that this had been a mistake and she became

convinced that women did need the vote, though she never became active in the movement. Mrs Humphrey Ward, on the other hand, did not waver in her views and, paradoxically, demonstrated in the leadership of various anti-suffrage societies that women had all the capacity for taking part in public life that the pro-suffrage women claimed.

One interesting index of the changing position of women was provided by the Nobel Prizes set up at the end of the 19th century: Mme Marie Curie shared the prize for Physics in 1903 and in 1911 won the Chemistry prize outright for her work of refining radium out of pitchblende and investigating related problems of radio-activity (only one other person, Linus Pauling, has won two Nobel prizes). In 1905 Baroness von Suttner was awarded the Peace prize, though to some extent this was just a compliment to Alfred Nobel, the dead founder of the prizes, because the Baroness had been his secretary for the last years of his life. In 1909 the Literature prize was awarded to the Swedish poet, Selma Lagerlöf; her writing was rather consciously elevating in tone and she concentrated on the sort of subjects thought suitable for women, such as the beauties of home life. The Literature prize is notoriously awarded, to a much greater extent than any of the others, on the basis of making sure that no important group feels left out, and the award to Selma Lagerlöf may have been intended as a compliment to women in general.

*Left: Women in the headlines: Isadora Duncan **(top left)**, the emancipated woman par excellence; Mrs Emmeline Pankhurst **(top right)**, protagonist of total war on anti-suffragist and neutral alike, and one of the greatest orators of her time; Marie Curie **(bottom)**, Nobel Prize-winner, together with her husband Pierre*

CORONATION OF WOMANHOOD

BALLOT BOX

FOR SHERIFF Miss HANG MAN

VOTE FOR The CELEBRATED MAN TAMER SUSAN SHARP TONGUE

Chapter 3
The Focus on the Suffrage

Although the position of women had changed in so many ways between the middle of the 19th century and the end, the question of votes for women had hardly moved. Between 1870 and 1890 there was no change at all but in the 1890s there were the first hints of a revival of interest. When Wyoming became a state of the Union in 1890, after a struggle with Congress, the women kept their votes. This meant the women would vote for Congressmen and for President. Until then women's votes in Wyoming had been the equivalent of unmarried English women's right to vote in municipal elections if they had the necessary property qualification. In 1893 the reforming Liberal-Labour government in New Zealand gave women the vote, and thus for the first time women had as much electoral power as men. Even this did not really have to be taken seriously: New Zealand was just a faraway scrap of the British Empire, and not a sovereign state.

The anti-suffrage forces drew their real emotional strength from a feeling (accepted as deeply by women as by men) that women were meant to be dependent rather than equal. However, when they had to provide arguments, they very often said that some areas of activity were particularly appropriate for women – they did not say that men should keep out of these areas, but they did assert that women should stick to them. The home, of course, was the real place for women, but it was accepted that in public life perhaps education and municipal affairs were also suitable for women.

This rationalised giving a few women municipal votes and letting them sit on school boards in England, though not on county councils.

The enemies of votes for women found it reassuring that the new idea was flourishing only in out-of-the-way places. In the 1890s three more states in the western USA joined Wyoming, and Western Australia and South Aus-

Top left: Pioneers of women's enfranchisement in the north-western states of the USA. Equality of the sexes was usual in the wild West. Bottom: American caricature of women voters

39

tralia (two of the smaller states) enfranchised women. It hardly seemed likely that the example of these distant areas, out on the frontiers of civilisation, would be followed by great and established governments like those of Great Britain, Germany, and the United States.

In one important way Australia, New Zealand, and the American West were typical of what the rest of the world was going to become. In Europe, or on the eastern seaboard of the United States, a woman could be a lady: what it mainly required was good manners and enough money to have servants. In the areas where women first got the vote it was notoriously difficult to keep servants. Girls who went out to the wilder parts of the English-speaking world found it so easy to get a husband that they had no need to go and work for someone else; their husbands could earn a living for themselves, but could never earn enough to employ servants. The decline in the number of servants has gone on at about the same rate as the spread of votes for women: the example set on the frontiers of civilisation, not in the drawing-room, has been followed.

Women and democracy

The people who wanted to keep women out of important political questions, and thought they ought to stay at home, usually also distrusted the capacity of other men to handle these problems. Determined opponents of votes for women tended to be more or less explicitly anti-democratic. Reformers said that if the voice of the people could be heard, governments would be nobler in their actions, and giving votes to women would have a particularly purifying effect. The more democratic the organisation, the more likely it was to include votes for women in its programme.

After getting the vote, women were a little more ready to vote for a conservative or right-wing party than men, but in the last years of the 19th century it always looked as though women were on the left in politics. In Russia, where the constitution was described as 'despotism tempered by assassination', the Nihilists were determined that assassination should become more frequent; they killed Tsar Alexander II in 1881, and they were a threat to Tsars and ministers for years to come. Women played a considerable part in their secret organisations and the enemies of the Tsar asserted that the political police always tortured women on a basis of perfect equality with men.

Top right: Belligerent women in New York parade for better working conditions. Bottom right: The House of Representatives politely receives a deputation of female suffragists, early 1871

'Red Rosa'

Until 1907 women in Germany were in theory not allowed to belong to political organisations, but this was not strictly enforced. The sternly Marxist Social Democratic Party was committed to the principle of equality, and was ready to practise it. Clara Zetkin rose to a position of importance in the party while it was still banned by Bismarck's legislation, and a little later she was joined by one of the most remarkable of all women who have gone into politics: Rosa Luxemburg ('Red Rosa', as she was nicknamed, to her disgust). Of course, she could not be elected to the Reichstag, but the Social Democrats attached little importance to the Reichstag because it had so little power, and regarded party conferences as the really central political activity. At conferences Rosa was in her element: she was a speaker of great power, a rigid Marxist, and a forceful logician.

Inside the party a few of her opponents tried to arouse feeling against her by pointing out that she was a woman, and Jewish, and Polish, but the Social Democrats were fair-minded and paid very little attention to any of these issues. Rosa herself found time, in the intervals of a great deal of work in Germany, to encourage the Polish and the Russian parties of the left. Votes for women she simply took for granted: obviously any socialist community would give women equality, but the important thing was to establish socialism and not allow reforming energy to be led off into the essentially bourgeois question of votes for women. This may have seemed rather harsh; however, it was what quite a number of men on the left believed as well. They accepted the principle of votes for women, but they were always afraid that it was going to be used to hold up other reforms.

The French parties of the left shared this worry about votes for women. By the beginning of the century a few Frenchwomen were beginning to stage demonstrations for the right to vote, and French reforming politicians all admitted that they had a good case. The Socialist Viviani raised the issue in the Chamber of Deputies for the first time in 1901.

The French Union for Women's Suffrage was launched under the leadership of Mme Braunsching, in 1909, but it did not make much progress. The Radicals were convinced that women would vote as their priests told them — too many freethinking Radicals had devout wives for them to trust women with the vote. The result of their conviction that votes for women would reinforce the parties of the right was that French women had to wait till after the Second World War to get the vote. And their assessment of the situation was not unjustified. When women did get the vote they supported the *Mouvement*

Républicain Populaire (MRP), which was the most consciously Roman Catholic Party. It was also the party most devoted to social reform without drastic changes in society, and this is the sort of political attitude that women seem to prefer – they are perhaps readier than men to respond to abuses and cases of injustice, but they feel that a radical change in society opens up the risk of disturbance and violence.

Change and the old order

In fact, the Church itself was rather hostile to the demand for votes for women, and felt that this would make them more independent and would break up the family. But more important than the hostility of the Church was the fact that in general the Roman Catholic countries had not become as urbanised and industrialised as the Protestant countries. As a result, at the beginning of the 20th century women were in a weaker position to ask for their rights in Catholic countries. And, it is probably also true to say, they were much less interested in asking for them.

So, by 1900, women had a good chance of getting the vote in urbanised, industrialised countries, where they could get office jobs and where servants were becoming difficult to find; in other countries the problem was not much discussed. But there was one other factor to consider, and it probably explains why votes for women caused so much trouble and disturbance in England.

In a new country, or in an old country when it undergoes great upheaval, change is relatively easy. Wyoming could give its women votes: it was giving its whole population votes for the first time. The other American states which gave women the vote in the 1890s were only just emerging from being territories and becoming states. By the beginning of the 20th century women's suffrage was accepted as the modern thing to believe in; every new country wants to be modern; and so every new country was sympathetic to votes for women. And an unexpectedly large number of new countries emerged in the 20th century. It was in older, established countries that changes were harder.

Left: A parade of hats at a suffrage meeting in Paris, 1908

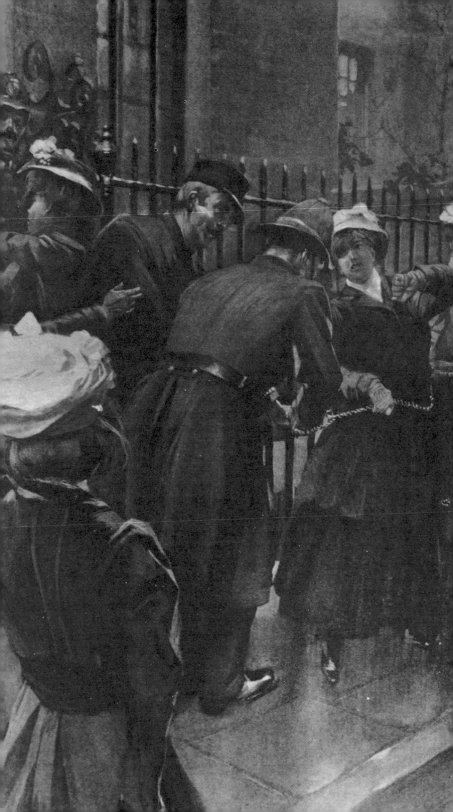

Chapter 4

Two Ways: England and Scandinavia

In England changes did take place, but they happened quietly and people tried to ignore them. But the question of votes for women – in fact, the whole question of women – was hard to ignore, and so it aroused opposition. Before 1900 it was still possible to ignore the question and opposition had not been violent or abusive. The National Union of Women's Suffrage Societies went about its work of lobbying, and MPs were polite to it. But in innumerable ways they could hold up legislation without actually voting against it: Henry Labouchère had voted for the original John Stuart Mill amendment in favour of women in 1867 but he had grown less liberal in his opinions, and in the 1890s he amused himself by holding up bills on women's suffrage by making a long speech on the item of business immediately preceding it on the order paper. This meant that the supporters of votes for women did not even get a chance to put their case, let alone get it voted on, and it also meant that he did not have to say anything against votes for women that might infuriate the women who wanted the vote and thus increase their fighting spirit.

In 1898 the radical Dr Richard Pankhurst died and left his widow Emmeline with four children to look after, and very little money. She found a job – life would have been much harder twenty or thirty years earlier – and she was encouraged by Eva Gore-Booth and a number of other women to take an interest in politics round Manchester. In October 1903 she started the Women's Social and Political Union. 'Social' did not mean that they were going to spend their time drinking tea; the WSPU started as an ally of the Independent Labour Party, and the Pankhursts were all socialists at this stage.

In 1903 the Conservative Party had been in office for eight years, and it was beginning to lose its grip. The next election was likely to produce a Liberal government, and with a Liberal majority in the House of Commons probably most of the MPs would be fairly sympathetic

Left: *The struggle becomes militant: suffragettes aggressively chain themselves to the railings of 10 Downing Street, 1908*

45

to votes for women. Sympathy was always worth having, but it was not enough. Under the English system of government a policy that was supported by the Cabinet was practically certain to pass into law, but if the Cabinet was not interested in it, or merely thought that other things were more important, ordinary MPs would not be able to do much.

The situation was quite different from that in the United States. There the President obviously had a great deal of influence, but the individual Senators and Representatives had a great deal of freedom of action. Each one of them was worth lobbying, and each one of them was aware of the fact. The tactics of the English National Union of Women's Suffrage Societies would have made better sense in the United States; Miss Lydia Becker, the tireless and devoted secretary of the NUWSS in the 1890s, had gone round and round the MPs lobbying them in a way that would have been very useful in Washington.

The tactics of sensation-mongering

The Pankhursts understood the English system rather better; they knew that to make progress they had to arouse public opinion and make people interested in the question. They may have realised that this would arouse hostility, but hostility was more useful than indifference. In October 1905 Mrs Pankhurst's eldest daughter Christabel and Annie Kenney, a mill girl who belonged to the WSPU, were arrested and charged with trying to cause a disturbance at a political meeting in Manchester. They were found guilty and offered the choice of a small fine or imprisonment. As their overriding aim was to attract attention, naturally they chose imprisonment. And they were noticed. The newspapers of course deplored their behaviour and said that this was no way to conduct political agitation, but the press had paid so little attention to the NUWSS that all the supporters of votes for women were glad that something had been done to make people pay attention to their cause.

The general election came at the beginning of the next year, and the Liberals duly won their enormous majority. A vast crowd of enthusiastic reformers, each with his own reform to suggest, poured into the House of Commons. To be successful a reform had to catch the eye of Liberal enthusiasts without upsetting the Liberal Cabinet. The Pankhursts moved to London immediately after the election and began preparing their campaign. They began by

Right: While events in England took a spectacular, embattled turn, support for the Cause stayed, in less urbanised France, at a less impassioned level. The lithograph by Juan Gris (1910) shows the comparative calmness of a French feminist meeting

organising a procession to the Prime Minister in Downing Street, starting from Queen Boadicea's statue on the Embankment.

The Prime Minister, Sir Henry Campbell-Bannerman, listened to them politely and said he approved of votes for women, but that his Cabinet was divided on the issue. The women then went away and held a large meeting in Trafalgar Square—they were already picking up the normal methods of agitation used by men, and were soon to go rather further. They began heckling Asquith, the Chancellor of the Exchequer, at his meeting because it was well-known that he was the centre of the opposition in the Cabinet which the Prime Minister had mentioned.

The pestering of Asquith by members of the WSPU led to arrests. Annie Kenney rang at his doorbell long enough to be a nuisance, and another of the besiegers of his house slapped a policeman in the face. The women were arrested, and again chose to go to prison rather than pay their fines; there was a little argument about whether they were being properly treated in prison, though this was nothing to the commotion that broke out in a few years' time over forcible feeding.

The WSPU seemed to have succeeded in arousing public opinion. Mrs Fawcett, the leader of the NUWSS, said that the WSPU had been more successful in getting people to pay attention to the women's movement in twelve months than her own organisation had been in twelve years. Though the two organisations were still on friendly terms, the difference of approach had been noticed; the supporters of the Suffrage Societies were known as suffragists, so it was natural to call their more violent allies in the WSPU 'suffragettes'. The latter name stuck, and by now almost anyone who supported votes for women in the days before the First World War is liable to be called a suffragette. But at the time the suffragettes were a very special group—they did not always like the nickname, and sometimes called themselves 'militants'—with a special approach to politics.

It is said that Gandhi noticed what was going on in England, and was inspired by it to use methods of civil disobedience, first to help the Indians who had settled in South Africa and later, on a much larger scale, in India itself. The methods of the suffragettes suited his needs very well, just as they have suited the needs of many other agitators in other countries, working for other causes. A government which gives its people freedom to make speeches is not likely to treat them very harshly if

Left: *The face of protest: arrest of an intransigent English suffragette. MPs were harangued on the terrace of the Commons from chartered river steamers by strident feminists*

they break the law in a more or less symbolic way (civil disobedience in a country where the government is ruthless in using its powers would be much more risky and has not been attempted).

The political prospects for women looked a little better by the opening years of the 20th century. The transition of the six states of Australia into the Commonwealth of Australia aroused a great deal of interest in politics, and this was accompanied by a willingness to give women the vote. Women who could vote in South Australia and Western Australia were allowed to vote in federal elections from the formation of the Commonwealth in 1901, and in 1902 all women were allowed to vote in federal elections. By 1908 women in the other four states had gained complete electoral equality. This was a distinct step forward: Wyoming, or even New Zealand, might be laughed off but Australia had to be taken seriously.

The Northern democracies

In Norway something comparable happened. Norway and Sweden were still united at the beginning of the century, but the two states had a fair degree of independence in local affairs. In 1901 Norway gave the vote in municipal elections to women on a property qualification. By itself this might not have been very important, but in 1905 Norway separated from Sweden.

The new country of Norway gave some women the vote almost immediately, and by 1913 they had complete electoral equality with men. The Scandinavian approach to women was already more relaxed and egalitarian than that of any other countries—when Isadora Duncan visited Copenhagen in about 1907 she noticed the 'extraordinarily intelligent and happy look on the faces of the young women, striding along the streets alone and free, like boys'. In fact women in the Scandinavian countries were winning more and more of the immediate practical issues for which the vote would have been very useful, but were winning several of them without the help of the vote.

Finland had been under Russian rule, but in many ways Finns held the same attitudes as inhabitants of the other Scandinavian countries. The Finnish Women's Association was an important part of the country's life, and was one of the organisations that kept alive the idea of a separate nation. When Russia was in difficulty in 1905 during her war against Japan the Finns took advantage of the situation and gained a good deal of internal autonomy. In 1907 Finnish women got the vote—the first country in Europe to put them on the same footing as men in elections.

Perhaps the most serious issue raised in the Scandinavian countries—though not only in those countries—was

what became known as the 'endowment of motherhood'. Ellen Key, a Swedish social reformer, argued that mothers should be paid enough by the state to enable them to do their job properly. The Swedish reformers were quite explicit that their concern extended to unmarried mothers. They pointed out that the chief victims of the harsh traditional attitude of society towards unmarried mothers were the children, who had done nothing wrong. The supporters of endowment of motherhood were not certain whether an unmarried mother really had done anything wrong, but for tactical purposes and to avoid shocking public opinion more than they had to, the reformers always spoke as though she had sinned, but had sinned as the result of a generous and trusting disposition.

There was probably something in this. By the beginning of the century a really well-informed woman might know something about birth control: when the secretary of the Fabian Society in England conducted a survey of the married members around 1905 to ask them if they were deliberately limiting their families, a large majority of them replied that they were. Of course this was a group which would be relatively hard to shock; very few of them declined to answer on the grounds that these questions ought not to be talked about, though most people at the time would have felt outraged at being surveyed in this way.

Even so, it is not clear what methods the members used to limit their families; they may simply have been practising high-minded abstinence. The arrangements in the Asquith family have recently been revealed by Sir Oswald Mosley, who tells the story of how Mrs Asquith called on Lady Cynthia Mosley: 'Dear child, you must not have another baby for a long time. Henry always withdrew in time, such a noble man.' But an ordinary simple girl at the beginning of the century might not have heard of any method of birth control, and yet if she became a mother her position was desperate. The death rate among children of unmarried mothers was very high, sometimes because the frantic mother killed her child, sometimes through neglect and a certain amount of cruelty in the orphanages to which unwanted children were consigned, and sometimes from simple poverty.

The great surveys of poverty carried out in England at the end of the 19th century by men like Booth and Rowntree showed that poverty and large families often went together. Some politicians became convinced that children's allowance ought to be paid, and this view gained a good deal of support on the continent of Europe. It was a reform which appealed to right-wing politicians as well,

Left: An English suffragette appeals to an all-male audience

because it would encourage expansion of population, and make sure that young children were brought up fit and strong, both of which would be useful for the large armies, based on compulsory military service, that were maintained in Europe. The idea was less successful in the English-speaking world; England and Canada waited until the end of the Second World War before introducing family allowances, and the United States has never accepted the idea. Anyway, these allowances have been intended to supplement the husband's wage and make it easier to bring up a large family. The idea that a mother had a right to receive payments large enough to enable her to bring up a family by herself is still more revolutionary.

H.G.Wells and the female heart

While the argument about 'the endowment of motherhood' was on, H.G.Wells wrote his political novel *The New Machiavelli*. It is remembered today for its venomous account of the home life, the meagre hospitality, and the unceasing political intrigues of Sidney and Beatrice Webb; and it was intended as a tract in favour of generous payments to mothers and attacking the institution of marriage. Wells in his personal life showed an inability to confine himself within the strict bounds of marriage – apparently one of the humorous sights at literary and political conferences in the 1920s was to see Wells with his close friend, the Baroness Budberg, hurrying along behind him – and in the context of the pre-1914 world he was seen as a liberating influence.

Bernard Shaw at the end of his play *Pygmalion* tidies some of his characters out of the story by explaining that they came across H.G.Wells and immediately all their social problems were solved. Not Eliza Doolittle's problems of course, which were only to be solved by a magnetic teacher with no real interest in women, which was basically Shaw's idea of himself; but the other, more middle-class young women in the play were, as Shaw realised, more suited for Wells's prescription than anything he could suggest.

Wells's novel *Ann Veronica* (autobiographical in its later chapters) may have convinced Shaw that Wells understood this particular problem. Ann Veronica was just the sort of girl to become a young and active suffragette; educated to do a job, working in a scientific laboratory, frustrated by the fact that her parents seem not to understand why she is so fidgety and anxious to go out into the world. The novel gave, among other things, a pen-portrait of Christabel Pankhurst and an account of imprisonment after a demonstration. But Wells was writing a romance rather than a political novel – there seem

to be no worthwhile novels about the suffragettes – and in the end Ann Veronica got her slice of real life by going off to live with a married man. The story had a happy ending; the man's wife disappeared and he and Ann married, to the intense and understandable relief of her parents.

Only a small number of people became suffragettes and broke the law or struggled with the police. The strength of the suffragettes depended on the fact that they had an army of supporters behind them who approved of votes for women – some of them girls suffering from Ann Veronica's type of frustration, but many older people as well. Some of their supporters regretted their methods, but their form of active agitation did not cost the cause any supporters for the first four or five years in which they were used.

Asquith – a formidable opponent

Advocates of votes for women suffered a nasty setback at the beginning of 1908. Campbell-Bannerman, a passive friend, retired from the premiership, and died almost immediately. His successor was Asquith, with his memories of being badgered by the suffragettes in the previous years. Asquith was too cautious a man, and altogether too skilful a politician, to talk about his reasons for opposing votes for women. His second wife, Margot, was brilliant but erratically clever; after he had been forced out of the premiership in 1916 she published her autobiography, which harmed him in his efforts to get back into power. Among other things it suggested that the Asquiths went on opposing votes for women even after the law giving them the vote had been passed.

Asquith was fond of his wife, but was quite unlike her. He had a neat turn of phrase, though he did not always use it in a way to win him friends. He once said, 'I am sometimes tempted to think, as one listens to the arguments of supporters of woman suffrage, that there is nothing to be said for it, and I am sometimes tempted to think, when I listen to the arguments of the opponents of woman suffrage, that there is nothing to be said against it': neither side can have been pleased by this assessment of the situation, though the opponents of change did have the satisfaction of knowing that Asquith was helping their side.

But the forces against him were impressive. The more

Left: A gallery of the first women lawyers (late 19th century).
Left from top to bottom: Marie Popelin (Belgium), Signé Silen (Finland), Jeanne Chauvin (France), Nanna Berg (Denmark).
Right from top to bottom: Four Americans – Clara Shortridge Foltz, Florence Cronise, Mary Greene, and Belva Lockwood

53

peaceful supporters of votes for women had organised a march in February 1907 — owing to the rain it became known as the 'Mud March' — in which about 4,000 people took part. Male helpers were called in to help: the rising economist Maynard Keynes acted as a steward, and the rising literary man Lytton Strachey ought to have been there but hurried away to Cambridge out of a feeling that he might be going to make a fool of himself.

Three days later the less peaceful suffragettes held a march. The procession was broken up by mounted policemen, who rode the women down with some ferocity. The London press could not take the suffragettes seriously, but it protested very firmly against this use of the police. The government began to be worried: it could not agree on a policy about votes for women, but it realised that clashes between women and the police, whether they did good or harm to the women's cause, could only damage the prestige and electoral position of the government. This thought was to trouble the government quite often in the next few years, but they found no solution to the problem.

*Top right: Norway — matriculation of the first female student at Christiania University, 1882. **Bottom:** Finland — pressure from the Finnish Women's Association results in electoral equality for women, 1907: the first European country to achieve it*

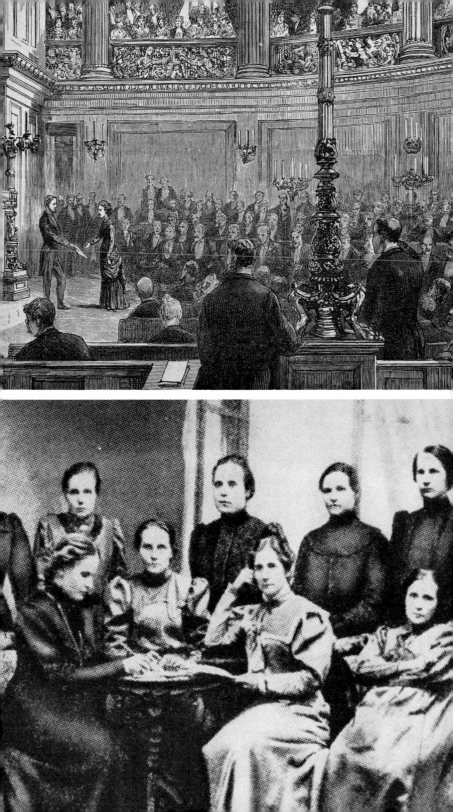

'The Screaming Sisterhood'

As a stirring topical theme, 'Votes for Women' was meat and drink to the cartoonist. That woman is always news is an old journalistic truth, but, now that she had become a natural subject for parody, caricature, and crusading idealism, the pencil became for a while mightier than the pen. **Below:** Many thought that an attractive woman was her own best spokesman and that femininity was enough. *Punch* magazine promoted the myth that 'women who wanted women's rights also wanted women's charms', that only the gauche and the ugly needed the artificial support of votes. **Top right:** Lloyd George's 'mewing cats'. The truculence of the suffragettes aroused deep masculine prejudices and fears of the danger of 'sacrificing one's manhood'. **Bottom right:** A poster issued by the Women's Social and Political Union: the logic seemed impeccable, but the consequences unforeseeable. Politicians equivocated and played uneasily for time. Nobody knew how women would vote.

AS THEY DR
THERE WER
AND THE B
FOR A TIM

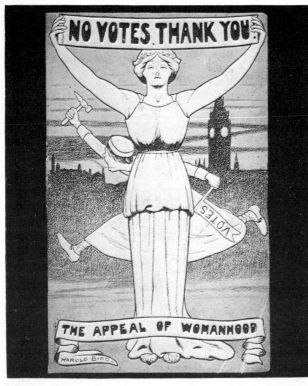

Chapter 5

The Advance of the Suffragettes

The opponents of votes for women did have one advantage, apart from Asquith's support. In England (as in the United States) votes for women could not be passed into law without affecting the rest of the political situation. In the United States there was the question of prohibition, and the fear of everybody in the liquor trade that if women had the vote they would ruin the trade. There was also the fear of the southern whites that if women got the vote it would be harder to keep a grip on the southern Negroes. Enough southerners remembered the explosive effect of Harriot Beecher Stowe's *Uncle Tom's Cabin* in arousing support for abolition of slavery to know that northern women were powerful and determined, and were remarkably hard to persuade that Negroes were getting a fair deal. In addition, there was the point of view expressed by the southern Senator who said that he reckoned they could always hit a Negro man on the head if he tried to vote, but he was not so sure that hitting Negro women would be acceptable.

The cross-currents in England were not so bitter, but they did hold up the pressure for change. The difficulty was that only about two-thirds of the men in England had the vote: only a householder could be a voter, and men who lived with their parents, or who lived in ordinary rented rooms or flats did not have the right to vote. Perhaps this should have consoled the women for being excluded, but its actual effect was to make it less likely that women would get the vote.

One simple proposal was to give the vote to everybody, man or woman, at the age of twenty-one. But the proposal was altogether too simple: no Conservative, whether he belonged to the pro-votes for women minority in the Conservative Party or not, wanted to see so many poor people added to the voters' list. The Conservative supporters of votes for women wanted to restrict the vote to women householders, and of course in practically every

Left: The Executive Committee of the International Council for Women meeting in July 1899: Susan Brownell Anthony, the American suffrage leader, is second from left in the front row

59

family the man was the householder. The Conservative approach would have given the vote to a small group made up of widows and spinsters of wealthy families (and, it was pointed out, to the more successful prostitutes who had acquired houses of their own, though there cannot have been many of them). The Liberals did not like this idea at all.

The women themselves did not really mind, at this stage, what approach was taken. They wanted to get some women on to the voters' list, and calculated that the rest would probably follow. If it had to be a limited Conservative-type franchise, they would put up with it. However, at this point the women in the WSPU were divided by an argument within their organisation which had very little to do with suffragette principles or tactics. Policy in the Union was controlled by the emergency committee, and the emergency committee was dominated by Mrs Pankhurst and her two daughters Christabel and Sylvia. They were the core of the movement, and would have dominated the Union whatever the constitution said, but some members challenged their authority and tried to make the committee more directly responsible to the membership.

A remarkable family

Mrs Pankhurst was a lady, and a lady of immense determination, considerable skill in speaking and in propaganda, and (as became clear later) no regard for her health, her safety, or her life itself, if they had to be sacrified for the cause. Christabel was a convincing answer to anyone who thought the suffragettes were dull or dowdy. She was very obviously good-looking, she had immense vitality, she had her mother's skill as a speaker; it was not quite so clear that she was a lady. Sylvia was fairly certainly not a lady. At first she wanted to be an art student and then she became convinced that something would have to be done for the poor. Because she was a Pankhurst she was a suffragette, but she was one of the few members of the WSPU who remembered that it had started off as a socialist organisation and felt that it ought not to become a feminist group with no other political commitments. This caused trouble later, but in the first of the WSPU's internal struggles she was firmly on her mother's side.

Mrs Pankhurst could probably have won the majority of the members to her side if she had asked for their support in the normal way. Instead she carried out a coup, seized control of the organisation, and imposed a new constitution. None of the suffragettes were meek and

Right: Sylvia Pankhurst speaking in the East End of London

mild, and those who were not devoted admirers of Mrs Pankhurst would not stand for such behaviour. They set up the Women's Freedom League; the main difference between it and the Pankhurst-dominated WSPU was that it did not believe in violence, but its members were quite ready to break the law by holding processions in defiance of the police and by refusing to pay taxes.

One great difference between the WSPU and all the other women's organisations was that Mrs Pankhurst had got her teeth into London and meant to stay there. The other organisations were strong all over the country; the WSPU was concentrated in London, and most of its violent and vigorous steps to publicise its cause were taken in London. This made sense; the suffragettes lived by publicity, and they wanted to gain the attention of the press. The British press was dominated by the London newspapers, and if the newspaper reported that a suffragette meeting had been broken up by the police in London, the whole country would soon hear about it. Comparable meetings anywhere else in the country would receive much less attention.

People at the time—especially Asquith and the opponents of votes for women—knew perfectly well what was going on. They also knew that the antics in London mattered only if they aroused enthusiasm outside London. A Miss New chained herself to the railings in Downing Street and started shouting 'Votes for Women' while a Cabinet meeting was going on. Until the police brought a hacksaw to cut the chains she went on shouting, and attracting so much attention that Mrs Drummond, one of Mrs Pankhurst's trusted lieutenants, was able to get into 10 Downing Street and shout 'Votes for Women' inside the Prime Minister's own house.

This sort of thing would not convince the anti-suffrage ministers but—apart from being great fun—it did attract the attention of other women and make them interested in the struggle. Miss Matters, of the Women's Freedom League, chartered a balloon and flew across London, dropping leaflets on the way: perhaps some of the leaflets reached the people who read them and were convinced, but the flight made sure that nobody could forget about the suffragettes. Some women tried presenting a petition to Edward VII when he was going to open Parliament; perhaps they thought he had some influence on these political questions, but the main point was to provide a public demonstration.

In the summer of 1908 larger processions were held than in 1907—and in better weather. In June the suffrage

Right: Mrs Charlotte Despard, socialist and pacifist chairman of the Women's Freedom League, speaking in Trafalgar Square

societies held a combined procession from the Embankment to the Albert Hall. They came in groups, artists, actresses, graduates, and writers, each carrying an embroidered banner to say who they were. Mrs Pankhurst led one section, the Women's Freedom League marched as another section, and the movement appeared united and harmonious.

The next weekend the WSPU put on a demonstration of its own: an open-air meeting at Hyde Park, at which it marked itself off from the other suffrage societies by adding a purple stripe to the white and green colours adopted by all supporters of votes for women. Special trains brought supporters to London, and *The Times* estimated that over 500,000 people came to the meeting – an improbably large number (for comparison, the Campaign for Nuclear Disarmament on some occasions got a crowd in the order of 100,000 to Trafalgar Square and the great civil rights demonstration in Washington in the summer of 1963, at which Martin Luther King made his 'I have a dream' speech, was estimated at about 250,000 people).

But even if the suffragette meeting was not as large as *The Times* said, it was still a distinct demonstration of their importance. And the government presented them a few weeks later with another opportunity to gain publicity. Mrs Pankhurst, Christabel, and Mrs Drummond were put on trial for conduct likely to provoke a breach of the peace at a meeting in Trafalgar Square. The three women were convicted, and were sent to prison after they refused to promise not to commit a breach of the peace again. Such a promise would probably have stopped them from organising any more meetings, so it was hardly likely that they would give it.

The campaign hots up

By 1909 it could be seen that there would be a general election, after the House of Lords had rejected the government's budget. Politics naturally became livelier, and the methods of the suffragettes became livelier to meet the occasion. When the Prime Minister went to Birmingham, his organisers found to their dismay that the only really large meeting-hall in the city had a glass roof; they rigged up a tarpaulin across it and when two women climbed up to the roof they were arrested before they could   **69** ▷

---

*Top right: Militancy provokes arrest after a scuffle round Nelson's Column. **Bottom:** Suffragettes march in their white 'injured innocence' dresses. Sylvia Pankhurst, aloft, leads the chanting. **Next page:** 'The Haunted House': a contemporary poster shows the House of Commons lying uneasily beneath the heavy, brooding and unwelcome menace of 'Votes for Women'*

THE HAUNTED HOUSE

smash the glass. Another woman tried to attack Winston Churchill with a dog-whip though he managed to take it away from her before she could injure him.

Women hid under the platform at meetings (and at the Albert Hall inside the organ) and jumped out shouting 'Votes for Women'; they continued to arrange large processions; and one woman locked herself into Lloyd George's car and gave him a long harangue on the importance of giving women the vote. But although the suffragettes had no reason to feel friendly to the Liberal government, they knew that a much larger proportion of the Conservative opposition was hostile to votes for women.

Hunger strikes

The government did not face the situation with equal satisfaction. Keeping the suffragettes in order became harder in 1909 when women in prison started going on hunger strike. At first any woman who seemed to be growing weak during a hunger strike was released. But this was too easy: any woman who had departed far enough from the conventions of the age to get arrested for a political demonstration was probably determined enough to go on hunger strike, and a policy of rapid release simply meant that all prison sentences would be reduced to a matter of three or four days. And the government would look very silly.

So the government had to proceed to forcible feeding. No British government could like this, especially a Liberal government which depended on Irish support. Some of the Irish MPs had themselves been in prison in the 1880s for political offences and several of them were sensitive about prison conditions. In any case this was a period of growing concern about prison conditions. Churchill, who was Home Secretary at this time, was particularly sensitive to charges that women prisoners were ill-treated. The story was told that he wanted to be quite sure that forcible feeding was as humane as his civil servants told him, and accordingly he arranged to be fed forcibly himself.

If the government was finding the struggle a little wearing, some members of the House of Commons were determined to bring it to an end in the only complete and final way, by passing an act giving women the vote. In 1910 a Conciliation Committee was formed, with members drawn from all parties, to produce a bill which could bring together all supporters of votes for women.

The bill they produced was an almost complete acceptance of the Conservative point of view, giving the vote to

Left: A suffragist poster pleads for an end to men's paternalism

69

women householders, including women who owned a piece of property which was not being used as her husband's qualification for voting. This meant that apart from the widows and spinsters (and perhaps prostitutes) who would benefit if women householders got the vote, the bill would also give votes to wives whose husbands had two homes. Naturally people rich enough to keep up two addresses usually voted Conservative rather than Liberal.

Lloyd George and Churchill opposed this particular bill on the grounds that it gave too much to the Conservatives, though they stressed their commitment to the principle. The debate was enlivened by Lord Hugh Cecil's statement that when voting 'I am not conscious of performing a function either difficult or sensational or particularly masculine. . . . It is a serenely tranquil, an austerely refined, and from beginning to end a thoroughly ladylike operation.' The bill got a majority on the second reading, but clearly was not going to get any further.

Deadlock had also appeared in national politics. Another election about the House of Lords had to be held in December 1910, and in this election Asquith softened enough to say that if the Liberals won the election they would produce a bill to widen the franchise. The more optimistic supporters of votes for women saw this as a virtual promise that they would get their way and that Asquith would withdraw as gracefully as he could. The election made little difference to the parties in the House of Commons, the Liberals remained in office, and early in 1911 the WSPU called off the campaign of agitation by violence. Peace and the hope of a reasonable settlement dawned in England, and Mrs Pankhurst went to North America to tell the story of the struggle.

Top right: Suffragettes freshly released from prison often retired to Eagle House, Bath, to recuperate. For everyone who stayed there a tree was planted in a special arboretum. Here Mrs Pankhurst (right) and Annie Kenney (left) pause for a break; Mary Blathwayt, the owner's daughter, is in the centre.
Bottom: Stirring times for the feminist vanguard in America

Chapter 6

Regrouping in the United States

The American suffrage societies had healed their quarrel over Victoria Woodhull, and in 1890 had formed the National American Woman Suffrage Association. But they had not done much more than this. In a country as large as the United States, with a federal constitution, organisation and co-ordination were vital; and they were nowhere to be found. In the four western states which had given women the vote, quite apart from the lack of servants or of a strong liquor interest, there were simply very few people to be canvassed; in the larger states the population was too large for the women's organisations to have much effect.

Some of the American suffrage leaders thought the best line of approach was to get Congress to initiate a constitutional amendment. Susan B. Anthony, the second president of the reunited NAWSA, was committed to this method; in the course of years the proposal became known as the Susan B. Anthony amendment, and eventually the form of words she suggested in 1875 was adopted forty-five years later. Because of the risk that the measure would get lost in the intricacies of Congressional procedure another group of leaders preferred to press the individual state legislatures which controlled voter qualifications. But a change on this scale often required a referendum to change the state constitution, and so the women who thought they could get the vote through the individual states found themselves plodding through a succession of campaigns that needed a great deal of organisation.

When Susan Anthony retired in 1900 she chose a woman a whole generation younger than herself to be the new leader of the NAWSA. Mrs Carrie Chapman Catt was ideally suited for the task of reducing the United States to a series of neatly indexed cards listing people who would work for votes for women, Senators and Representatives who would support it, people who could be **77** ▷

*Left: Campaigning for women's suffrage in the USA. The bystanders show amused tolerance. **Next page:** NAWSA, presided over by George Washington, prepares for the dawn*

organised to help, and people whose opposition would have to be met and overcome. This operation was necessary but not exciting; after she had spent four years making the machinery efficient she retired, to be replaced by Dr Anne Shaw who was an inspiring orator, a less efficient organiser, and a dozen years older than Mrs Catt.

Dr Anne Shaw did not do much better than Mrs Catt. The question looked dead in 1900, and for another decade no progress was made. But Mrs Pankhurst's visit in 1911 came at a moment of great hope and change; between 1910 and 1912 another six states gave women the vote by referendum. All ten women's suffrage states were in the west, all of them except California were inclined to be dry, and most of them either had a state-wide Prohibition law or passed one in the next few years.

Cautious advance

The women could not hope for much progress in the south. The southern ideal of a lady made no allowances for her taking part in politics, and southerners had no desire to see anyone extending the franchise at any time. So the women had to concentrate on the cities of the east if they were to make any progress. The women who wanted the vote were inevitably middle-class and almost equally inevitably Anglo-Saxon. They were also inclined to dislike Negroes and immigrants, because Negroes and immigrants were the backbone of the strength of the machine politicians and the machine politicians were usually against giving women the vote. The attitude of the party machine was shown in Illinois in 1913: the legislature allowed women to vote for the President of the United States, but did not allow them to vote for Congress or for state office; and, of course, the reason was that the machine was not much worried about Presidential elections, but was concerned about the less important positions.

New York was an even harder proposition than Illinois. A Women's Suffrage Party had been launched there, and it made some progress by taking a liberal line on questions of social reform. Votes for women received a great forward thrust from the Triangle Fire in 1911; an unsafe building, full of badly-paid garment workers, caught fire and 146 of the workers were burnt to death or killed when they jumped from the upper floors. Opponents of votes for women pointed out that there were many unsafe buildings in New York in which men might be burnt to death even though they had the vote, but the fire

*Top left: The aftermath of the Triangle Shirt Fire, 1911, which aroused widespread sympathy for reform. **Bottom left:** Suffrage 'hikers', 1913: staunchly respectable pilgrims spread the Cause*

77

aroused interest in a wide range of reforms and women's suffrage benefited along with the others.

The great parades

Some of this enthusiasm showed itself in the form of great parades. New York, and American cities in general, were more accustomed to parades and marching organisations than English cities, but the New York parades in 1912 were spectacular enough to attract attention from the most jaded audience. People came to jeer, but on the whole the city was tolerant enough and in any case the marchers were obviously highly respectable and were well-ordered and well-dressed; the whole thing was very reminiscent of elegant marches with embroidered banners in London half-a-dozen years earlier. Women picketed the party conventions that year, and arranged parades in several cities.

A parade in Washington was organised in March 1913 when President Wilson was inaugurated, and the orderly, tidy procession began its march. But it was held up by an anti-suffrage mob, and the police (who had given a permit for the march) made very little effort to help it go on. The riot that followed had the effect that might be expected: the women had been badly treated, and a great many people who had come to Washington for the inauguration had seen that they had been badly treated. Sympathy for the women turned into support for giving votes to women.

The 1913 riot in Washington, and the reaction in favour of women, was a great encouragement to American women who wanted to show that they too could fight for the vote. Mrs Pankhurst's visit had been at a time of truce in England; by 1913 the struggle in England was raging much more fiercely than ever before, and this inflamed the struggle in the United States as well. Two young Americans who had been working with the suffragettes in England, Alice Paul and Lucy Burns, rapidly rose to positions of importance after they came back to the United States; they controlled the Congressional Committee of the NAWSA and at the same time they launched their own Congressional Union — as the names suggest, they were firmly committed to making progress through Congress and forcing it to accept the Susan Anthony amendment to the constitution.

They believed that the methods of the suffragettes could be transplanted across the Atlantic and used in Washington. Perhaps they were right, but the NAWSA certainly did not think so; the sensational approach might

Right: The gathering momentum: suffragette parades in Washington **(top)** and Greenwich Village, New York **(bottom)** 1913

78

be all very well in England, but in America respectability should be the keynote of the campaign. Within the year Miss Paul and Miss Burns had been pushed out of the Congressional Committee, and Dr Shaw's position as President was weakened because she had supported the two newcomers.

But the pair of them still had their Congressional Union, and it quickly became the American equivalent of the WSPU. Mrs Belmont, one of the wealthiest women in the United States, supported it with her money, partly because her ex-husband William Vanderbilt opposed votes for women. It quickly took the name of the Women's Party and by 1915 it was organising groups throughout the country. But the NAWSA had no intention of being pushed aside; it quickly reorganised itself, Dr Shaw retired from the Presidency and was replaced by Mrs Catt, which showed that the members felt that stricter discipline and less oratorical inspiration were needed.

Despite the NAWSA's efforts to revitalise itself, in 1916 the Women's Party was certainly succeeding in attracting attention. Apart from parades and struggles with the police, they began picketing the White House. President Wilson was understood to be favourable to votes for women, and at first he smiled politely and raised his hat. But the suffragettes went on to chain themselves to his railings; this was not as effective as in Downing Street, because there is a large and pleasant lawn between the railings and the White House, but it still showed that the suffragettes were determined to attract attention.

Even so, their demonstrations in the United States never reached the level of raw fury seen in England in the years immediately before 1914. The Women's Party upset the NAWSA; and naturally a good many people who wanted to escape the polite lobbying of the NAWSA would assure the ladies who visited them that it was all the fault of the suffragettes who were making such a fuss – the NAWSA always took refusals of this sort at face value, and blamed the Women's Party, but probably a good many of the people who gave this excuse were implacable enemies of votes for women who did not want to publicise the fact.

Left: Mrs Emmeline Pankhurst seated in front of Mrs Belfont, the New York suffrage leader. The Cause attracted supporters from rich high society (top left), and even the men got in on the act with a League for Women Suffrage, in New York (bottom)

Chapter 7
The Struggle in England Resumes

The situation in England, which had looked peaceful and likely to end quietly when Mrs Pankhurst visited North America in 1911, had slipped out of control quite quickly. The first step came in November 1911 when Asquith announced that his government was just about to introduce a bill that would give votes to all adults, and he said that amendments to give votes to women would be discussed. If the Commons voted for them, the government would not make any difficulties.

Mrs Pankhurst, still in North America, denounced this as treachery, which must have looked like an unnecessary willingness to resist any attempt at conciliation. The suffragettes opposed the government's approach because the fiercer members of the WSPU wanted a separate act of Parliament giving women the vote, and did not want to be enfranchised simply as an afterthought in a bill primarily concerned with giving more men the vote.

Mounting violence
The difference between giving women the vote in a bill which was all their own and lumping them in with the men started the whole struggle off again. Before Mrs Pankhurst had got back to England from North America there was a great scuffle between the police and a procession of suffragettes in Parliament Square – 200 women were arrested. When Mrs Pankhurst did get back she invited her followers at a mass meeting to go out and break windows: 'We don't want to use any arguments that are unnecessarily strong. If the argument of the stone, the time-honoured official political argument, is sufficient, then we will never use any stronger argument.'

Before this threatened escalation took place, there was another and more violent – almost final – quarrel between the suffragists and the suffragettes. A large and respectable meeting of suffragists was held in the Albert Hall, with Lloyd George as the main speaker and Mrs Fawcett the suffragist leader as chairman. The suffragettes came

Left: Lady chauffeur in Downing Street demonstration, 1911

83

and shouted at him and called him a traitor, and although the meeting was not broken up it was harder for suffragists to feel sympathy for the suffragettes afterwards.

A week later Mrs Pankhurst's notion of an official political argument was put into effect. At four o'clock in the afternoon of 1st March 1912 a well-disciplined group of 200 women broke most of the windows in the smart shopping area round Piccadilly Circus and along Regent Street and Oxford Street; some of them brought bags of stones for this, and the better-equipped had come with hammers so that they could go on attacking several panes one after another. Mrs Pankhurst herself went to Downing Street to throw stones – not a sensible arrangement, for she was a notoriously bad shot.

The 200 window-breakers were arrested, and the government also decided to arrest the other WSPU leaders. Christabel heard that the police were coming and left quickly for Paris, but Mr and Mrs Pethick-Lawrence, two other prominent WSPU members, were arrested at the WSPU headquarters in Clement's Inn – not a tavern but one of the elegant lodging-places for lawyers and professional people near the Law Courts.

Leadership divisions

Mr Pethick-Lawrence (later Lord Pethick-Lawrence, a Labour peer) was one of the few men to play an active part at any stage in the women's agitation. Many husbands were willing and eager to support their wives in their actions, and several politicians were ready to speak on behalf of votes for women, but very little of the organising work in the movement was done by men. Most of the campaigns waged to give the right to vote to people who were previously unenfranchised have been led by enthusiasts who already have the vote, as in the struggles for the successive Reform Bills in 19th-century England, and in the struggles to get Negroes the vote in the United States. But the women did all their own organising, as pictures of committees and conferences will show. Mr Pethick-Lawrence's position, as the treasurer and fund-raiser of an extremist society, was unique. The WSPU was very good at raising money and had a substantial balance at the bank, as was proved at the trial of the leaders. It put out its magazine, *Votes for Women,* and paid the expenses of a number of full-time organisers. Its militant and aggressive policy does not seem to have frightened away subscribers, and probably attracted people to give money by being the organisation that was most visibly fighting to get the vote.

The three leaders were sentenced to nine months in prison, and although the sentences were shortened as

much as possible — partly because they went on hunger strike — this interval gave them time to reconsider their position. For the parliamentary situation had changed, in an ominous direction. A month after the window-breaking demonstration the House of Commons rejected a more wide-ranging version of the Conciliation Bill which had been dropped in 1910. The upholders of respectable lobbying and discreet pressure said that this defeat showed that window-breaking cost the cause votes where they really mattered. The admirers of the suffragettes claimed (and claim to this day) that the bill was defeated for quite different reasons: they pointed out that the Irish MPs had changed their minds and voted against the bill, presumably because they thought it might complicate the parliamentary timetable and hinder their darling project of Home Rule for Ireland; and that some MPs preferred to wait for Asquith's bill to give votes to all men to be discussed, because they understood it could be amended to include women as well.

While the Pethick-Lawrences and Mrs Pankhurst were in prison, the campaign was run from Paris by Christabel. The faithful Annie Kenney, who had been in the militant movement from the beginning, slipped across the Channel to see her every week and picked up instructions for the next move.

The swing to extremism
When the imprisoned leaders came out, the results of their meditations could soon be seen. The Pethick-Lawrences suggested that the suffragettes should not go any further in attacking property; Mrs Pankhurst obviously disagreed, and soon showed that she wanted the movement to go in for arson. She expelled the Pethick-Lawrences from the WSPU on her own authority and announced that she and Christabel would now be the sole leaders; the Pethick-Lawrences, who had been editing *Votes for Women,* kept their paper but Christabel launched a new and more militant paper, *The Suffragette.* The expulsion of the Pethick-Lawrences was much more amicable than the expulsion of the Women's Freedom League leaders five years previously, but the suffragettes were still to be regarded as a military movement, and the commands of the leader were to be obeyed without discussion.

This was an odd attitude for the leaders of a political agitation to take, but then the whole atmosphere of discussion was becoming very odd. Sir Almroth Wright, a

Left: Forcible feeding of a 'hunger striker'. At least one prisoner was driven insane by the methods used: a tube was thrust up the nostrils by one doctor and food poured down it by another

doctor of some distinction, wrote a very peculiar letter
to *The Times:* he suggested that half the women in the
country went mad to some extent as a result of the meno-
pause, and he made it clear that he regarded militancy
as a symptom of mental illness. He wrote: 'There are no
good women, but only women who have lived under the
influence of good men.' And he said that some of the
suffragettes had a programme which was 'licence for
themselves or else restriction for men'.

The suffragettes did not put the question quite like
that. Some wanted restriction; some wanted licence. In
The Suffragette Christabel Pankhurst wrote a series of
articles on venereal disease, later published as a book,
The Great Scourge. By the standards of the time it was
undoubtedly outspoken; but venereal disease was a
menace, and Christabel was doing a service to the
community in pointing it out. During the First World
War, when the wastage of men owing to disease was reducing the effectiveness of the army, the book was re-
printed as a guide and a warning. Although she blamed
the strict sexual morality of the time and the consequent
resort to prostitutes for much of the trouble, she made it
clear that she was not advocating free love or any anti-
cipation of marriage. As she put it in the introduction,
the programme was 'Votes for Women and Chastity for
Men', a much more elevated attitude than the one attributed to the suffragettes by Sir Almroth Wright. Votes
for women, in Christabel's idea of the future, would lead
to a strict enforcement of the laws against prostitution
by punishing the men who went to prostitutes as well as
the women themselves.

The insistence on chastity for men was not just a question of dealing with venereal disease. The 'double standard' of morality, which laid down that sex outside marriage was a trivial indulgence for men, and perhaps a
sign of virility as well, while it was an indelible disgrace
for women, was a clear sign of the inequality of the sexes
and the way that women's position was inferior. Christabel's approach was stern and puritanical; on the more
extreme fringes of the women's movement was a magazine called *The Freewoman* which was committed to the
freer varieties of free love. 'To the healthy human being
there is something repugnant in long-continued sexual
relationship with a person with whom one is in the constant and often jarring intimacy of daily life' and 'I
repeat that sterilisation is a higher human achievement
than reproduction' must have left the respectable Miss
Pankhurst feeling that the suffragette cause had quite
enough difficulties already without getting mixed up with
views like this.

The opponents of votes for women also had their ex-

tremists. Mrs Humphrey Ward, the anti-suffragist leader, felt she had to apologise for Sir Almroth Wright's letter (which, of course, had had the effect of convincing a good many women that the suffragettes were right). People had been saying odd things about women for a good many years: Lombroso, one of the earliest criminologists, had said 'even the normal woman is a half-criminaloid being' and the *Saturday Review* had called educated women 'vermin'. But there was now an increase in the number of odd things said.

Support from the Labour Party

With people in this sort of mood they were not likely to reach a friendly compromise at all easily. The struggle was growing more heated when George Lansbury, a Labour MP, became convinced that the government's treatment of women was intolerable. The Labour Party had about forty MPs at the time, most of them committed to votes for women. In 1912 the party conference laid down that no extension of the right to vote would be acceptable unless it gave votes to women — a startling commitment, because the Parliamentary Labour Party would be committed to opposing the government's forthcoming bill and resisting the efforts of the Liberals to enfranchise just that section of the population which would be most likely to vote Labour unless the bill included votes for women. So the Labour Party had arranged for itself a position where it might eventually be obliged to do its best to cut its own throat.

Lansbury however was no man for delay: he went out to cut his own throat immediately. He denounced the Prime Minister in the Commons: 'You are torturing innocent women.' Then in November 1912 he resigned his seat and stood again at the by-election as a women's suffrage candidate. In 1910 he had been elected by the efforts of the local Labour Party organisation, helped by the Liberals putting forward no candidate; at the by-election in 1912 some of his Labour supporters saw no need for a new election and the others got on badly with the WSPU.

The suffragettes felt that, as he was standing for their cause, they should run the whole campaign, but naturally they did not know the East End constituency of Bromley and Bow which he represented. If the suffragettes had worked with the existing organisation, Lans-

Top left: The apprehensive wait before final release. **Centre and bottom:** *A French view of feminists in operation — in England, hounding ministers* **(centre right)**; *in Germany, speechifying* **(centre left)**; *in Russia, terrorising* **(bottom left)**; *in France, most successfully, wearing the trousers* **(bottom right)**

bury might have won. As it was, his supporters did not get on together, and right at the end the WSPU motorcars were not made available to bring known Labour voters to the polling stations. Lansbury was defeated and the cause of votes for women suffered, though all that the defeat really showed was that the WSPU and the Labour Party did not have much in common. Sylvia Pankhurst believed in socialist principles, and stayed on in the East End, but the main body of the suffragettes went away convinced that an alliance with the Conservatives would be a good idea. And the suffragette hostility to legislation to give votes to poorer men – because they wanted women to have a bill all to themselves – looked like a pro-Conservative attitude.

Asquith's betrayal?
But at last in January 1913 Asquith's bill to give votes to all men was to be debated, and the supporters of votes for women prepared a series of amendments to put women in the bill. There was a day of debate on the women's suffrage amendments; some Cabinet Ministers spoke for the change, others spoke against, for the issue was treated as an open question, in the way that capital punishment has been treated at Westminster in more recent years. Next day the Prime Minister asked the Speaker what would be the effect on the bill if an amendment giving votes to women was passed. The Speaker then gave his ruling: the bill was supposed to be to give votes to men, and if the women were brought in, the amendment would be so fundamental that the whole structure of the bill would have been overturned. Accordingly, if the women's amendments were passed, an entirely new bill would have to be introduced.

Asquith said politely that the government's bill and the promise that amendments could be introduced had been based on a misunderstanding; the government would withdraw its bill. Asquith said that there had been no sharp practice but inevitably the suffragettes did not believe him and they were convinced that he had known all along what the Speaker would do.

Within the women's movement the effect of the fiasco was to strengthen the position of the Pankhursts. They had cried out for no compromise and no amendments, they had said that the government was not to be trusted and was no true friend of votes for women, and they had been proved right. The WSPU attracted supporters away from the decorous constitutional societies which had believed in the good faith of the government. The Pethick-Lawrences appeared as weak-kneed in their opposition to a drastic policy. The next step up from breaking windows was – it had always been obvious – for the suffra-

gettes to turn to arson. And in the early months of 1913 they did just that.

Arrests for arson

They burnt a couple of rural railway stations, they placed a bomb in the house being built for Lloyd George at Walton Heath in Surrey, and they wrote 'Votes for Women' in acid on the greens of some golf courses. And these attacks were meant to hurt; previously women who had been breaking the law, whether in a peaceful way by marching in a procession without police permission, or violently by breaking windows or trying to force their way into the Commons, had intended to be arrested in order to show that they took their beliefs seriously, and to make a speech from the dock in defence of their beliefs at the trial. But by this stage the suffragettes were no longer looking for opportunities for martyrdom. They wanted to fight against society.

They were sometimes caught by the police, and in any case there were still some less violent demonstrators trying to get arrested in what had been the normal way. The government took fresh powers to deal with the problem caused by hunger-striking; the 'Cat-and-Mouse' Act allowed the Home Secretary to release any prisoner who had gone on hunger strike, but then to bring her back to complete her sentence when she had recovered her health. Naturally the mice declined to co-operate; once a hunger-striker was out of prison she usually tried to elude the police. Mrs Pankhurst was something of an exception; she was constantly being rearrested under the 'Cat-and-Mouse' Act, and as constantly being released because she had been reduced by her unceasing efforts to a state of weakness where a day or two on hunger-strike made it necessary to release her. The government was naturally terrified that she would die; it would be worse if she died in prison, but if she died anywhere the government would be blamed and the suffragettes would carry on the fight with more fury than ever. Her death would not even remove the leader of the organisation, because Christabel safely in Paris was now planning the struggle.

A martyr for the cause

In June 1913 Emily Davison went to the Derby at Epsom, and threw herself in front of a group of horses by Tattenham Corner. She could not have picked out which horse to run in front of, though it happened to be King George

Left: Martyrdom snowballs. Top: Arrest and demonstrations. Bottom: Emily Davison's death at the Epsom Derby, 1913. 'The Cause has need of a tragedy,' she said on one occasion

V's horse Anmer. The jockey was thrown, but recovered; Emily Davison died of her injuries four days later.

To bring her body back from Epsom to the Davison family grave in the north of England, the coffin had to be taken from Victoria to King's Cross. This was one of the largest of all the processions for votes for women; there were supporters of the cause in black or purple or white, groups of women arranged by profession, and embroidered banners, all reminiscent of the days of peaceful demonstrations half-a-dozen years earlier. It was primarily a WSPU procession—Mrs Pankhurst was not there, for she was rearrested as soon as she stepped out of her house to take part, but women who had no sympathy with the campaign of violence could respect Emily Davison's death and find for a short time the unity and agreement that had been lost under the stress of militancy.

It was a brief respite; the WSPU soon returned to the attack. It was still dominated by the centralising tendencies of Mrs Pankhurst and Christabel; at the end of 1913 they told Sylvia to stop her activity in the East End of London, and return to the main stream of suffragette agitation. Sylvia's East End movement was becoming increasingly socialist in tendency. Christabel and Mrs Pankhurst may have felt that it was difficult enough to run a militant campaign for votes for women without going in for socialism as well, but pretty certainly jealousy and snobbery also entered into it: Sylvia was building up support among working-class women that was devoted to her rather than to the other two Pankhursts, and the other two were meeting such a lot of smart women in the cause of the struggle that they felt Sylvia was lowering the social standing of the family by going off and living in the slums.

Sylvia was not noticeably more peaceloving or accommodating than the rest of the family. She refused to give up her work, and the other two expelled her from the WSPU. But she continued with her own organisation—it ran on a smaller scale than the WSPU, because Sylvia had to combine the roles undertaken by her mother and her elder sister in the larger organisation. She worked out the plans, but she was also the martyr for the cause, constantly being arrested, going on hunger-strike, being released, and returning to the struggle. She was carried round on a stretcher, almost always with a large group of her East End housewives accompanying her and this bodyguard helped her to escape rearrest on a number of occasions.

By the beginning of 1914 suffragette tactics were becoming increasingly frantic. They went on setting fire

Right: Suffragette marchers mobbed and beaten in Wales, 1912

to houses, and they took to attacking pictures: the Rokeby Venus in the National Gallery was slashed, and so were a number of other less valuable paintings. The suffragette policy was to do anything as long as it was not a threat to human life—of course, if they had kept up the policy of arson, sometimes by using home-made time-bombs, sooner or later someone would have been killed and this would probably have led to a public reaction against the movement.

Lesbian undertones

Although the public resented arson and destruction, it also resented the methods used by the police. The suffragettes who were arrested and put on trial did not lack public sympathy; the demonstrations were accepted as a sign that some women were in deadly earnest. The morale and unity of the suffragettes were high: some historians, notably George Dangerfield in his *Strange Death of Liberal England,* have suggested that there was a strong tinge of lesbianism about the more militant suffragettes, but this is greatly exaggerated. Undoubtedly Christabel herself was not interested in men—though she was not as suspicious of them and their motives as the respected Susan Anthony in the United States—and it was perfectly true that many of the young militants were passionately devoted to her as their leader. In a period before Freudian analysis had made people self-conscious about their relations with members of the same sex, they could express this devotion more openly than people could do at the present day without wondering about the sexual implications of what they were saying.

Probably several active and determined girls of lesbian inclinations would join the suffragettes, but there is no real sign that they were an important part of the movement. Habits of dress provide some misleading evidence. Despite the passing of the crinoline, fashionable women's clothes had not become any less restricting and repressive, and changes in fashions in the decade before 1914 did nothing to make life easier.

Any woman who wanted to establish her position of equality with men at that time would tend to wear severe and mannish clothes; at the present day such clothes may indicate a lack of interest in men, but in the years before the First World War many women wore these clothes simply to show that they were serious-minded enough to qualify for a job. Women's fashions of the time were clearly not practical for earning a living; if a woman was going to earn her living she almost inevitably adopted a costume closely resembling that of the men among whom she worked, with, of course, the exception that she would wear a fairly long skirt.

Dangerfield supports his view about lesbianism by referring to the enthusiasm of some of Christabel's Parisian friends for the poems of Sappho. These people were not active suffragettes, and, in addition, Sappho was and is accepted as the greatest of all women poets. Any woman who was committed whole-heartedly to the cause was bound to have a great admiration for the Greek poet: almost all her writing consisted of very unrestrained love-poems to the women who lived with her, but probably this was much less important for the suffragettes than the fact that she was a woman writer who had triumphed over the handicaps placed on her sex and had become a great artist.

The type of solidarity felt by the militants was expressed by Annie Kenney, who wrote, 'No companionship can ever surpass the companionship of the militants,' and by Rachel Ferguson who wrote, 'The suffrage campaign was our Eton and Oxford, our regiment, our ship.' These comparisons made very good sense: there had not been many opportunities for women to work together, and the emotional climate of the suffragette campaign was raised by this sense that they were doing something new. Undoubtedly a good many of the hard core of determined militants found the years of conflict before 1914 the most exciting period of their lives. The youngest of the suffragettes are now in their seventies, but for most of them the time of struggle is still a happier memory than almost anything else in their lives.

This emotional satisfaction—sexual or lesbian only in a very remote sense—was very real to the suffragettes, but it could hardly affect the policy of the British government. In the years of extreme militancy the House of Commons voted on women's suffrage more seriously than before; Private Members' bills were introduced in each session. They were defeated by fairly slender margins, and a good many opponents of the bills were simply waiting for the government to take a position. A bill to extend the franchise was likely to be introduced to take the place of the one laid aside in the 1913 fiasco; many supporters of the government waited to see what form this bill would take before doing anything to help votes for women forward.

In June 1914 Asquith agreed to see a suffragette delegation. Not a WSPU delegation but a group from Sylvia

Top left: The Daily Herald *points the fresh turn of events: 'The New Advocate* **(left)** *refers to Emily Davison's death; 'Why don't they forcibly feed us?'—a comment from a slum child* **(right)**. *Bottom left: Emmeline and Sylvia Pankhurst in prison. In one year Sylvia withstood ten successive hunger-and-thirst strikes: she was fed by stomach tube twice a day*

Pankhurst's East London Federation for Women's Suffrage. Poor women, who had to look after a family and at the same time earn a little money to help the husband's wages go further, came into Downing Street to see the Prime Minister. They explained what Parliament could do for the problems of poor working women, and they made a considerable impression on Asquith.

Previously he had felt that the suffragettes were a lot of rich women making a fuss because they wanted something to do—also he had, not surprisingly, been very upset when a group of them tried to tear his clothes off when they ambushed him during a visit to Scotland. As a party leader it was his business to wonder what the electoral implications of the change would be; the more he saw of the WSPU and its steady tendency to climb up the social scale, the more he must have felt that votes for women meant votes for the Conservative Party.

But the women of the East End on the delegation were not of this sort. In straightforward electoral terms, they were likely to vote Liberal (or to turn to the infant Labour Party). In social terms they had a case; the government could do something about some of the handicaps under which they suffered; if they had the vote, they would be less likely to be overlooked. Asquith did not commit himself completely, but he went a long way towards saying that the government would bring in a bill to give votes to everyone, men and women.

The WSPU were not in the least pleased by this. Quite apart from their understandable feeling that things had gone wrong once in 1913 and might go wrong again, what Asquith had suggested was a bill for men and women, and they wanted one for women alone. So the suffragette attacks went on for another six weeks. The whole scene was transformed in August by the outbreak of the First World War; the women's organisations plunged into the war effort, with the WSPU leaders most prominent in patriotic activity and most ready to forget about the struggle to get the vote.

Right: Mrs Pankhurst is arrested outside Buckingham Palace. At her trial she said: 'I look upon myself as a prisoner of war' Next page: A British programme advertises a demonstration against women's suffrage (left), while (right) a suffragist poster draws some damning electoral parallels. Women's suffrage remained a burning issue until the First World War closed the ranks. Ironically the first female MP to sit in the House of Commons was to be the American-born Nancy, Viscountess Astor, in 1919: ironically, because, far from being an agitator, she was actually surprised to find herself 'the first parliamentary shot to be fired by the great cannon of the women's movement'

ROYAL·ALBERT·HALL

NATIONAL LEAGUE FOR OPPOSING WOMAN SUFFRAGE

VIOLET MARKHAM

Demonstration

AGAINST

WOMAN
SUFFRAGE

Under the
auspices of the

NATIONAL

LEAGUE

for

OPPOSING

WOMAN SUFFRAGE.

THE RIGHT HON. EARL OF CROMER, G.C.B., O.M., G.C.M.G.

Photo by G. C. Beresford.

28th February,

1912,

AT 8 O'CLOCK IN

THE EVENING.

THE RT. HON. EARL LOREBURN

HON. LEWIS HARCOURT, M.P.

LORD WEARDALE

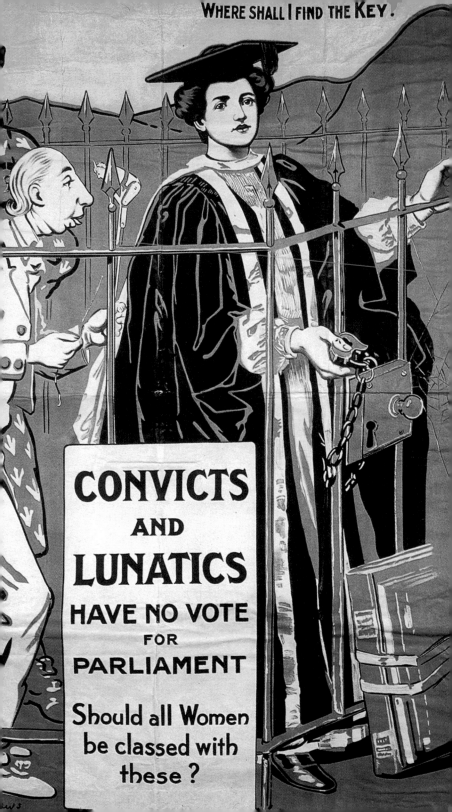

Chapter 8

The Great War

At the end of the war, when women were enfranchised (along with men) in the 1918 Representation of the People Act, it suited a lot of people to talk as if women had been given the vote simply because of what happened during the war. This does not seem very plausible; the emotional stress in England in the years just before the war was much higher than it was anywhere else during the whole long history of women's struggle to get the vote, but the women in England had been part of a movement that was gaining ground all over the world before the war — in many places inspired by the struggle in England and the Pankhurst example of leadership and self-sacrifice, which may have looked even nobler seen from afar.

The initial effect of the war was probably to delay the coming of votes for women in a few places — Asquith's response to the East London Federation suggests that English women would have got the vote in 1915. But while the war was on, there was not much change: Denmark (which at that time included Iceland) gave votes to women in 1915, and the Netherlands did so in 1917. In 1917 some women in Canada were given the vote, by an unpleasant device considered by a number of countries after the war.

The suffrage movement had not been strong in Canada before the war. Despite attempts by groups with British and groups with American connections, there was not much response. Canada was not highly urbanised, and the large Catholic section in Quebec was traditionally-minded and showed every sign of resenting the 20th century. To the normal Catholic feelings in favour of women remaining devoted to family life, there was added the political calculation that if they raised large families the Catholics of Quebec might become numerically dominant in the electorate — ('la revanche des berceaux' or 're-venge through the cradle').

Canada entered the war without doubts or misgivings, but it was soon clear that English-speaking Canada was

Left: *Workroom of a British war hospital supply depot, First World War. Girls of genteel background could now feel useful*

far more whole-heartedly committed to it than French-speaking Canada. The demand for manpower became so intense that Canadian units could not be kept up to strength without conscription, but by this time Quebec was no longer ready to co-operate. Most of the Liberals from outside Quebec joined the Conservative government to impose conscription; the anti-conscription Liberals were obviously going to win almost every French-speaking seat in Quebec. The Coalition government needed to win every seat it could in English-speaking Canada, and it passed a Wartime Elections Act which, apart from measures like disenfranchising immigrants from Germany or Austria-Hungary, gave votes to women with husbands or other close relations in the forces. It could be taken for granted that they would vote for the Conservatives, simply to make sure that the war effort was maintained and their relations at the front were not deserted.

All women were given the right to vote in nation-wide elections the next year — provinces could make their own rules and while all the others had enfranchised women by 1922, Quebec waited until 1940. But the Canadian example of differential enfranchisement, based on war service, was adopted after the war by Belgium (which did not give universal suffrage until after the Second World War), and was considered in a number of other countries.

The vote and post-war regimes

When the war was over, it turned out that defeat in battle was what really helped the cause of votes for women. In Russia women got the vote in 1917 when their country was collapsing under the weight of the attack from Germany and Austria-Hungary and, whatever the other aspects of Communism may be, it has all the time been a noticeable feature of life in the Soviet Union that women are closer to equality with men than in most other countries outside Scandinavia. In Sweden, which had been neutral during the war, the parties of the left had opposed Germany, and the parties of the right had been pro-German. In November 1918 the parties of the left organised demonstrations in the streets of Stockholm, which pointed to the possibility of revolution, and to pacify them the government carried out several reforms in the next two or three years, including giving women the vote.

In 1918 Germany and Austria-Hungary themselves collapsed, and their Emperors were overthrown. Votes for women came naturally when the Weimar Republic under the Social Democrats was set up in Germany. Austria-Hungary disintegrated into the various national

groups which had only been held together by the rule of
the Habsburgs. Most of the successor states gave women
the vote in the course of the next three or four years.
In Austria, Hungary, Czechoslovakia, Poland, and the
three Baltic countries of Latvia, Lithuania, and Esthonia
(the northern half of the Austro-Hungarian Empire and
the western extremity of the Tsardom) women had got
the vote by 1923. This was not because there had been
a flourishing women's movement before the war but
because these new countries, building their constitutions
without any traditional limitations on their freedom, were
anxious to show that they were up-to-date and giving
women the vote was one way of doing so. This meant
Hungary and Poland, which would not immediately have
been placed on any short list of advanced and liberal
countries, appeared to be more favourable to women than
countries of western Europe like France and Italy. Under-
standably, in Balkan countries like Greece and Bulgaria
votes for women made little progress; the status of women
had been so low before the war that they were not given
the vote even in Yugoslavia, where a new country was
being put together and a new constitution was produced.

But France and Italy showed that even in advanced
countries, if there was no violent shock to the political
system, women would not get the right to vote unless
they organised a powerful body of opinion. Roman
Catholic influence could hardly be blamed for the resistance; in 1919 Pope Benedict XV commended the cause of
votes for women. The question was discussed in both
countries just after the war; it was passed by the French
Chamber of Deputies in 1919, but the Radical party's
fear that women voters would be influenced by the Church
meant that the women's cause lost the support of some
people who might have been expected to be on its side.
The measure was delayed, and eventually was rejected
in 1922 by the Senate for the first but by no means the
last time. In 1936 Blum's Popular Front government ap-
pointed three women under-secretaries in the ministry,
although they did not have the vote and could not sit
in the Chamber, but liberalisation got no further before
1939.

In Italy the question was discussed in the first few
years after the war, but Mussolini's seizure of power in
1922 ended any prospect of an improvement in the position of women. The rise of Fascism and Nazism was a setback to the women's cause all over Europe—ingenious
male political theorists might argue that Communism
and Fascism were just the same thing but the Communist

Left: *German comments on the way in which the war created
new jobs for women, and so prepared men for post-war changes*

countries did bring equality for women, and the Fascist rulers believed in Church, children and the kitchen for women *(Kirche, kinder und küche).*

Women's war work

The two real triumphs for agitation were in England and the United States. To be sure, women did play an important part in the war in both countries, but then they played an important part in the war in almost all the countries concerned. For the first time a war was being fought in which nations could bring out their whole capacity for working and fighting. The efforts of English women have been studied more than any others, because the English were anxious to show that it was by war service that women had earned the right to vote, and other countries were not so concerned about this side of the case.

If the work of English women can be covered in detail, it must not be forgotten that in other countries women were taking up new types of work; in France this was not so easy, because a great deal of the new work undertaken by women was to replace men in the factories where armaments and explosives were produced. So many French factories were in the part of France that had been overrun by the first wave of the German advance in 1914 that French women did not have so much opportunity to take on new jobs. In Germany the jobs were more available, and of course it was in Germany that women suffered most during the war — except in the sense that all women suffered from the deaths of men at the front — because Germany was in the grip of a tight blockade imposed by the Royal Navy and the German government was not good at planning how to deal with the domestic effects of the blockade. Substitutes were provided for explosives and for metals that used to be imported, but the food supply deteriorated, everybody was underfed and most people were hungry. In the absence of an effective rationing system, women spent their time queuing for what there was to buy.

Quite apart from the English desire to show how much women had done in the war, the situation changed much more in England than in any other European country during the war. The other countries had conscript armies, and knew that when war broke out most of the young men of fighting age would go away and would have to be replaced. No such arrangements had been made in England; millions of volunteers responded to the great poster of

Top left: *English women at war work. Queen Mary entered in her wartime diary: 'Worked from 3 to 5 planting potatoes. Got very hot and tired.'* **Bottom left:** *Tramway girls in Milan*

Kitchener pointing a warning finger and saying 'Your Country Needs You', but nobody had thought very much what would happen next. Even when conscription became necessary, people had not really worked out what to do.

For the first twelve months or so, the position of women in England was more or less unchanged by the war. The slogan 'business as usual' was launched by *The Daily Mail,* partly because women were being put out of work in the early stages of the war. Servants were being paid off, dress-making and the other demands of the social season provided much less work than usual, and at first there seemed to be no other jobs to do. But steadily the effects of the surge of volunteers into the army began to be felt, and so did the increasing demands for munitions. More shells were needed to blast a path through the German lines. Women who had been out of work now found it fairly easy to get jobs, often under better conditions than ever before. People admired the women who went off to work in shell factories, pouring liquid TNT into the canisters, running the risk of being blown up or – less drastic but still unpleasant – being stained bright yellow by picric acid. No doubt some of the munitions workers were making a sacrifice for the war effort; however, many of them had been doing more uncomfortable jobs for equally long hours, at lower wages and with much less security of employment, in the years before the war.

Women who had never previously worked did not often go into factory jobs, though some of them set up canteens in the factories as part of the war-time tendency to improve working conditions. But many more nurses were needed than before, and many of the new recruits were women from the comfortable classes who felt that they were now doing something useful; it was an unfortunate side-effect that their willingness to work for low wages encouraged everybody to think nursing was a vocation for which a living wage was quite unnecessary.

The woman whose fate attracted more attention than any other during the war was Nurse Cavell. She stayed on in Brussels when the German invasion overran Belgium. She and her nurses looked after wounded soldiers of all nationalities, but she also helped English and French soldiers to escape, usually to Holland where they were interned and could not return to fight. Helping soldiers escape was a violation of the rules evolved in order to give nurses some official position and immunity in battle, and no doubt she deserved some sort of punishment. But the Germans shot her – unchivalrous and inhumane, and unwise as well. She did indeed say 'Patriotism is not enough' but she also said 'I am glad to die for my country' and the execution certainly helped the

104

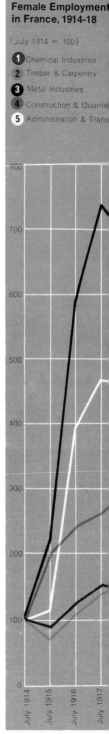

Index Numbers of Female Employment in France, 1914-18

(July 1914 = 100)

1 Chemical Industries
2 Timber & Carpentry
3 Metal Industries
4 Construction & Quarries
5 Administration & Trans

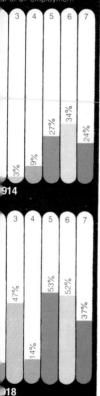

**ortion of Female to
 Employment
 UK, 1914-20**

ustry
nspod
ernment Establishments
 culture
nce & Commerce
al Government
al of all employment

British war effort. The Germans had been accused of atrocities in Belgium, but nothing was easy to prove because the Germans were in control in Belgium. Now the Germans had shot a nurse in Belgium many of the other stories looked more probable.

As the war went on it became more and more necessary to take a rational attitude to the supply of manpower, and very often this meant getting women who could take on work done by men. Women continued to take on office jobs, at a time when there was more and more office work to be done, keeping up with the forms and official documents which are an inevitable part of modern war. There were women bus conductors—cartoonists and photographers made a great fuss about them, though in fact there had been a few before the war. Women had always worked on farms; now 'land girls' from the towns volunteered to help on farms for the war effort and they were a great deal more use than the pessimistic farmers had thought they would be. England was never as short of food as Germany in the war, but the risk of submarine blockade was there, and more food had to be grown.

And women went closer to the battle than this. The women's auxiliary services—quite distinct from nursing—provided a range of services from lorry-driving to running field-telephone systems. The war showed that women could do almost all the jobs that men did. Before the war they had been slowly moving forward into almost every sort of work, but nobody noticed it or wondered what happened next. The war, when women at work suddenly became a vital part of the nation's efforts, showed men that life had changed, and made them ready to do a certain amount to accept the change.

Success at last

The idea of enfranchising all adult males, which the Liberals had been considering without too much enthusiasm in the years before the war, now became something that obviously had to be passed into law. And it was almost equally obvious that votes for women had to come as well. The suffragettes had laid down their stones and their matches and their chains as soon as war was declared—several of them equipped themselves with white feathers instead, which they thrust with indiscriminate fervour at men not in uniform, sometimes insulting men back from the trenches and making skilled munitions workers give up their factory jobs (in which they were hard to replace) to go off and fight. The militant spirit had not disappeared; it had just found new

Left: Diagrams illustrating the influx of women into men's jobs in the United Kingdom and France in the First World War

channels through which to flow. If votes for women had been refused, the spirit of the suffragettes could quite easily have arisen again.

The committee, under the chairmanship of the Speaker of the House of Commons, which worked out the principles for the 1918 Act, saw that there were more women than men in the population – mainly because of the pattern of births, partly because of losses in war. The men were alarmed by the idea of a female majority in the electorate; facing a comparable situation fifty years previously Gladstone had argued for an expansion of the electorate by saying 'they are our own flesh and blood', but the Speaker's Conference was more suspicious. It suggested that all men should be given the vote at twenty-one, and that women should get the vote at thirty.

Many of the leaders in the struggle for the vote did stand in the 1918 election, but none of them were success-ful – most of them stood as Labour or Liberal candidates in opposition to Lloyd George's Liberal-Conservative coalition government. Christabel Pankhurst was given a fair, but not a good, chance: she contested Smethwick, as a Coalition candidate with the support of Lloyd George. She was defeated by the Labour Party candidate though she polled more votes than any other woman standing.

One woman was elected in 1918, though for reasons which had nothing to do with votes for women. Countess Markievicz (born Constance Gore-Booth, sister of Eva Gore-Booth, who had helped set Mrs Pankhurst on the road to revolutionary action) was an Irish nationalist, who had come quite close to being executed for her share in the Easter Rising in Dublin in 1916. In 1918 she was elected as the *Sinn Fein* candidate for South Dublin. Like the other *Sinn Fein* MPs, she did not go to Westmin-ster but took her place in the *Dail* which declared itself to be the legal government of Ireland. When the Irish Free State had won its independence, it allowed women to vote at the same age as men. The age discrimination remained in force in England until another act was passed in 1928, though by that time all the excitement had gone out of the fight.

This was a silly little tailpiece to the struggle for the vote in England, caused by the foolish belief that all the women were going to vote for women candidates and swamp the men. Women are a majority of the electorate in a good many countries, but nowhere do they have any-thing like a majority of the seats in Parliament, Con-gress, or representative assembly. Several new classes of people have won the right to vote during the last hundred and fifty years, but very few of these new classes

Left: *Contrasts of peacetime and wartime industry in France*

have followed up their success by going into politics. Negroes make up almost a tenth of the electorate in the United States, but have nothing like a tenth of the seats in Congress; the manual working class make up between a half and two-thirds of the electorate in England, but have nothing like half the seats in the House of Commons. And women, who were an excluded class in just the same way as the Negroes and manual workers, are no more likely to end up with as many parliamentary seats as their numbers in the population would suggest.

America plays for time

The last important stage of the struggle for votes for women came in the United States. In the Congress elected in 1916 there was a clear majority for votes for women — obviously any Senator or Representative who came from the state which had given women the vote was going to support votes for women whenever it came up. This gave women a form of pressure on Congress which was more useful than the election of a woman Representative — Jeanette Rankin from Wyoming was elected for the first time in 1916, and she did show people that a Congresswoman was not an impossibility.

However, in the restricted undercover struggle in Congress she was probably a bit of a handicap for the supporters of votes for women. Her strong pacifist convictions made her vote against the decision that the United States should join the war against Germany in 1917, and this was not popular. It was used by some opponents of votes for women to suggest that the suffragettes were unpatriotic; the NAWSA had laid down that its members could take whatever side they chose about the war, but the accusation had some effect. Besides this, she had to take an important role in the suffrage debates because she was the only woman in Congress, but because she was new to the job she did not know all the pitfalls that had to be avoided. The enemies of votes for women relied on fear of the unknown to hold their votes united, and the task inside Congress was to soothe them and show at least some of the opponents that their fears were unjustified. Jeanette Rankin had not had enough practice at the job to know how to go about soothing the doubters.

A clear majority was not enough. The NAWSA had accepted the policy of the Susan Anthony amendment (and the policy of the Women's Party, though they would never say so) of getting Congress to present a consti-

Left: Not only did the war create opportunities for women, it also caused scarcities on the home front, as 'The Food Queue', a pastel by C.R.W. Nevinson, illustrates. In both ways attention was drawn to the needs and grievances of women

tutional amendment to the forty-eight states. If Congress accepted an amendment to the constitution by a two-thirds majority, then the states would have to hold special meetings of the legislatures to discuss the amendment. In these special meetings opponents would not be able to use procedural devices to stop the subject being discussed; they would have to come to a vote and declare themselves. All sorts of people who thought votes for women were undesirable would not care to say so in public—in particular, politicians would be afraid to vote against it, if they thought women were soon going to get the vote. Naturally, the more hostile to women a politician was, the more likely he was to think that they would be vindictive once they had got the vote and would throw out everybody who had been seen to vote against their cause.

So, once the amendment was through Congress, it would probably not have much more trouble, outside the South. The difficulty was to get Congress, and in particular the Senate, to do anything. At the beginning of 1918 the House of Representatives voted for the amendment by 274 votes to 136—a two-thirds majority, but the very barest two-thirds majority, and it is fairly certain that some Congressmen did not vote against the amendment but hoped that the Senate could do something to stop it. The House of Representatives is not easy to stir into action, but at least it does have ways of getting a vote if a clear majority wants one. The Senate has even more ways of avoiding a vote, and only a two-thirds majority can force one.

So the opponents of votes for women conducted a delaying action. This was a bit of a gamble. State after state was changing its own constitution and enfranchising women, and each such change meant that the Senators from the state became committed to votes for women unless they had made up their minds to retire from politics. Besides, American women were playing their part in the mounting war effort, and this provided fresh arguments for the supporters of change. There was nothing like the Second World War 'Rosie the Riveter' to suggest that women could do any job a man had done before the war, but women were needed as nurses, and as the United States committed itself to providing a vast modern army a great many men were summoned from their work and their jobs had to be filled.

No doubt some of the people who changed their minds and said that women ought to have the vote because they were doing so much in the war were just looking for a polite excuse to switch from one side of the fence to the other. Still, some men had simply not realised how much the world had changed in the previous fifty years; if the

LA COV RS

sight of women going to replace men called away to become soldiers helped these people to see how large the change had been, then the war did help the cause of votes for women.

The final stages in America

The activities of the Women's Party at this stage pretty certainly handicapped the cause. All through 1918 supporters of the change tried to get a few extra votes in the Senate and at the same time tried to get the Senate to come to a vote. The backbone of the Senate came from the South – courteous and determined old gentlemen who were afraid of the future but not unwilling to be reassured about it. President Wilson tried persuading a few of the more malleable Senators to see things his way; he could appeal to them as fellow-Democrats and point out that, while they might be safe for re-election, the party needed to show it was friendly to women to secure its position in Congress and to elect a Democratic President.

The Women's Party continued to apply the methods of the English suffragettes at a time when they were quite out of place: women chaining themselves to railings and screaming were exactly what the Southern Senators were afraid of. The Women's Party thought it would be fun to burn Wilson in effigy; in fact the police stoppped them making fools of themselves, but it was not at all clear what burning him was meant to do. Of course, if he had had the power to get the amendment passed and had been holding it up – in short, if he had been in the position of Asquith five years previously – it would have been understandable that the suffragettes were cross with him. But Wilson did not have the powers of the English Prime Minister (as he had pointed out with more than a hint of regret in his books on the American constitution) and he was doing the best he could for votes for women.

Eventually, in the last few weeks of the Congress elected in 1916, the Senate came to a vote, and the constitutional amendment was not able to get the two-thirds majority it needed. But in the new Congress, which had already been elected, there was a large majority for the amendment in the House of Representatives, and the opponents felt more ready than ever to leave the work of resistance to the Senate. But in the Senate a spirit of caution was at work. Not many people changed their minds, but a dozen or so Senators stayed away. Those who stayed away but were really opposed to votes for women were of course making it easier for the amendment to get a two-thirds majority, which it did in June 1919.

Left: The New Womanhood of France and Germany flexes its muscles: (top) at sport, (bottom) in the coal and shoe industries

111

The last stage, getting the state legislatures to confirm the amendment, took another fourteen months. Most of it went easily and smoothly, but the opposition still had some hope in New England and the South. By March 1920 the struggle had, appropriately enough, come down to a border state: Tennessee seemed the best immediate hope of finding a thirty-sixth state and passing the Susan Anthony amendment to the constitution. But the Governor of the State had no desire to see the matter discussed; he knew that the losers were going to be bitter after the fight, and he was not so sure that the victors – whichever side they were – would be grateful. The result of his delay was that the legislature did not meet until August, the hottest month of the year, when temperatures would make every man and woman wilt.

A vast band of lobbyists descended on Nashville to encourage the legislators to see things their way. Prohibition and the Volstead Act, which defined intoxicating liquors as beverages containing 'one half of one per centum or more of alcohol by volume', were already in effect, but nobody took the slightest notice. The NAWSA lobbyists claimed to be surprised at the sight of legislators going round drunk; in fact they probably knew what would happen, but thought it would be useful to tell everyone else what nasty people the opponents of votes for women really were. The supporters of votes for women reckoned they had the votes, and they also had the backing of the federal party organisations, neither of which wanted to look less enthusiastic about votes for women than the others. So the supporters of the constitutional amendment wanted the Tennessee legislature to keep cool hands and vote quickly; the opponents wanted to delay things, and the more muddled and fuddled they could get the legislature the better for their side.

But after a couple of weeks of this the legislators wanted to go home; and they passed the Susan Anthony amendment by 49 votes to 47. The NAWSA leaders went to Washington to see the signing of the official Proclamation of the Amendment. They were too late; the official responsible for the Proclamation had not wanted any further delay and as soon as he heard that Tennessee had voted he issued the document, without waiting for the victorious women's leaders.

Top left: Sergeant-Major Flora Sandes, 'the only British woman in the Serbian army'. *Bottom left:* German poster asks women to save their hair – for the war effort. *Left:* Berlin's first female butcher: anything a man could do, a woman could do too

113

Epilogue

And so the struggle was over. In the next twenty years about a dozen countries gave women the vote—most of them Latin American countries where the vote was often frustrated by military revolutions. The vote recognised women's equality, but really it came too late to help do much about it. If women had had the vote in the 19th century, they could have used it to help themselves forward in many struggles for economic advance and for the right to enter professions; as it was, they had to fight their way forward without the help of the vote, and in fact were able to do so with considerable success. In a way, the vote came after the battle had been won, though the struggle for the vote was one way for women to remind men—and to remind themselves—that they were not being given an equal chance. Efforts to stop women getting the vote were an attempt to pretend that nothing had changed in the 19th century and that women were still willing to live at home or to be overworked and underpaid.

If votes for women, by the time they were granted, were a monument to past progress, another event in 1918 —the publication of Marie Stopes's *Married Love*—was a pointer to the future. By present-day standards it is a very mild and unexciting book (only by an effort of historical imagination can one see why the British Museum had special arrangements for people who wanted to read it). But when it came out it was sensational: the witty and sophisticated Lady Diana Manners, who had been the leader of a little group that called itself the 'corrupt coterie', found it immensely worthwhile, and recommended it to her friends; the book had enormous sales and ran into legal problems on the grounds that it was outspoken on subjects that ought not to be discussed.

The book gave a simple account of intercourse and of contraceptive methods, presented Dr Stopes's theory of

Left: Japanese factory women hold a meeting to demonstrate against starvation wages. The ability to earn an independent living was in urban countries almost a precondition of suffrage

the times at which a woman would be most enthusiastic about sex, and stressed the fact that it was the husband's duty to make sure that his wife was in a receptive frame of mind. The success of the book does suggest that a good many married couples were still in the state indicated by the legendary mother's advice to the young bride: 'Lie still and think of England.'

Acceptance of the fact that women could expect something more than this in marriage, and acceptance of the fact that women do not necessarily have to get married first, have been among the larger changes in the position of women in the last fifty years. But there have been a great many others; equality in sexual matters has been among the most-widely discussed, but it rests on equality, or at least on greater opportunity, in a whole lot of other areas of life. 'Man must work from dawn till set of sun, but woman's work is never done' had some grim truth when sewing was done by hand, sweeping and brushing was done by hand, and when all rooms were heated (if at all) by coal fires and almost all meals were cooked by coal fires.

Middle-class comforts

Changes in these respects were coming in the years just before 1914 – Margot Asquith installed a bathroom in 10 Downing Street, which does not mean that Asquith was the first clean Prime Minister, but simply that water had previously been carried to the bedrooms by the servants and then carried down again. Gas and electricity for heating and for cooking, electricity for sewing-machines and vacuum cleaners, meant that women had less work to do, and what had to be done took less physical effort. These changes were beginning to affect middle-class homes at just about the time that the struggle for the vote was getting going: it was after women had got the vote that these benefits began to spread down to the working-class.

Possibly if women had had to choose between electricity and the vote, they would have been wise to choose electricity, though of course the choice never came in those terms. Once the vote had been won, it served mainly as a defensive weapon; politicians, and men in general, knew that there were some things they could no longer get away with, though on questions like equal pay for equal work they could hold their position for many years to come. Although they might not be going to do anything positive with their votes, women valued them for their defensive power, and took it for granted that the vote was worth having.

The story of the struggle for the vote almost inevitably concentrates on developments in the rich and advanced

nations. For example, the existence of office-jobs which gave women a fair chance of earning their own living at a middle-class level in big cities was an important factor in the spread of the suffrage movement. These jobs hardly existed outside the North Atlantic area and Australia and New Zealand. Outside these fortunate areas the right to vote was often denied to men as well as women; even in areas like Latin America, which theoretically believed in the right to vote, the harsh reality of the military *coup d'état* was almost as common a way of bringing about a change of government. When men did not care so much about the right to vote women were not going to press the point.

Progress in traditional societies

In the less prosperous nations, rich women were locked up, poor women were beasts of burden and there was no middle class to speak of. The ways in which rich women were locked up varied from continent to continent. In Latin America the influence of the Church, the duenna system, and a strict application of a double standard of sexual morality for men and for women combined to keep rich women strictly confined to private life. The harem system in Moslem countries, purdah in India, and the complex Chinese ceremonies of which foot-binding (wrapping up ladies' feet in tight bandages so that they remained delicately small, at the cost of crippling the women) is the best known, all had the same effect.

Of course, only the rich could go in for these elaborate performances. The women of the poor had to work, and wore themselves out in work and constant child-bearing just as in the more prosperous countries. The difference was the absence of any large class between the rich and the poor.

For a good many years the women's best hope of progress in these countries was that men were anxious to imitate the customs of the prosperous and dominant North Atlantic countries. People who wanted to be up-to-date all saw it in terms of following the pattern set in the West, and votes for women was part of the pattern.

Other customs had to change: respectable women had worn the veil in almost all Moslem countries, as a sign that they were cut off from the world outside their homes. Reformers like Atatürk in Turkey and Zaghlul in Egypt opposed the veil as one symptom of the backwardness of their countries – when Egyptian women showed that they had taken one step towards emancipation by coming out into the streets of Cairo in 1919 to demonstrate against

Left: Indian suffragettes, 1911. Women's suffrage was often a by-product of successful anti-colonial nationalist movements

British rule, Zaghlul reminded them of another aspect of emancipation by tearing the veil off one of the demonstrators.

For politicians living under colonial rule and trying to reduce its power, 'freedom' was naturally the leading slogan. Freedom from colonial rule for men, and also a bit of freedom for women. In English colonies women's political equality was recognised after 1918 and when men got the right to vote women also received it, usually on the same terms. In India, Burma, and Ceylon women got the vote as a natural result of the national movement towards independence.

In the independent country of Turkey women got the vote (fairly certainly to the disgust of the majority of male and female voters) because Atatürk saw this as part of his struggle to bring his country into the modern world. Of course, a small group of women appreciated the change; the sort of women who went to International Women's Suffrage Association meetings were glad that progress had been made, but obviously they were a tiny minority who could not have brought about the change by their own efforts. Even if they had been as determined as the suffragettes in England it would have done them little good; the militant suffragettes depended on the support of a large body of sympathisers, and the progressive women of Turkey (and a great many similar countries) would have found very little support among their country-women.

In a few Latin American countries women got the right to vote around 1930. Countries like Brazil, Cuba, Uruguay, and Ecuador were reasonably prosperous, and were willing to imitate the United States by giving votes to women. There was something rather haphazard about the process: in Mexico and Argentina the vote spread slowly on a province-by-province basis and in Chile, which was as developed as any of the others, women acquired the right to vote only in municipal elections.

By the late 1930s women had the vote pretty well all over the world, and it was seen as an inevitable development, though people were taking their time over doing anything about the inevitable.

Since the war
The Second World War, another war for democracy, established the point beyond all argument. Almost every European country was shattered by the war and had to start all over again by establishing a new constitution, and nearly all of them gave votes to women. An exception still remained: Switzerland had not been shaken by either war, and remains unshaken to this day. Swiss women are independent and are rather well-paid but still they have

118

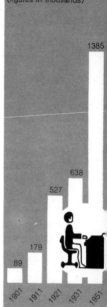

Female Office Workers in Great Britain 1901-1961
(figures in thousands)

1385

638

527

179

89

1901 1911 1921 1931 1951

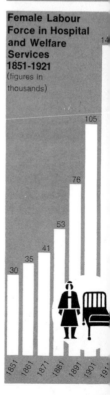

Female Labour Force in Hospital and Welfare Services 1851-1921
(figures in thousands)

14

105

76

53

41

35

30

1851 1861 1871 1881 1891 1901 191

**ale Labour Force
e Clothing Industry
-1921**

(s in thousands)

825
792
759
667
602
594
06

01 1871 1881 1891 1901 1911 1921

**ale Labour Force
e Textile
stry
-1921**

(s in
nds)

870
795
745
726
701
6

01 1871 1881 1891 1901 1911 1921

the vote in only a few cantons. They have made a little progress in the 1960s but in some ways the vote has not seemed very relevant; nobody would say that Swiss women are noticeably less free than French women or Italian women, both of whom got the vote in the aftermath of the Second World War. Scandinavian women are more free than any of them, but this is because of the cultural background and attitude to life of people in the Scandinavian countries rather than because women there have had the vote for a long time. Women in Australia have had the vote longer than women in Scandinavian countries, but they are probably less likely to be treated as equals by men than women in England or the United States. On the American frontier women were expected to do the same sort of work as men and keep the light of civilisation burning as well, but in the frontier conditions of Australia women had no real place. The Australian idea of mateship was for men only, and votes for women was the triumph of political ideals that did not correspond with men's real social attitudes. No criticism meant of Australia: the Australian example cheered and inspired many people to work for votes for women when the cause looked far from hopeful in the rest of the world. But if the equality that women wanted was something more than political, the vote was not an effective way of getting it (though nobody has found a better).

Women politicians of today

None of the women who took a leading part in the struggle went on to have distinguished political careers. Christabel Pankhurst never got into the Commons, and after a while she (like Victoria Woodhull and Annie Besant before her) took up a spiritualist form of religion. Jeanette Rankin was defeated for Congress on account of her vote against going into the First World War, and did not return to Congress until the 1940 election. Her pacifist ideals, held as firmly as ever, led her to vote against going into the Second World War, with the same result. At the age of eighty-eight she has taken part in protests against United States policy in Vietnam.

More recently several women have managed to go into politics with greater success. One woman Cabinet Minister seems to be about the quota in most of the countries where they play any noticeable role in politics, though American Cabinets (which are fairly small) usually contain no women and in England there have recently been two women together in the Cabinet. Ceylon was the first country to have a woman Prime Minister,

Left: Diagrams illustrating the pattern of female labour in Britain, where economic indispensability was crucial to the vote

when Mrs Bandaranaike was elected; it is fair to say that she had originally been chosen as leader of her party as a tribute to her husband after his assassination. In India there is a woman Prime Minister: Mrs Gandhi is perhaps the best person that could have been found for the job and it is no disrespect to her (it is more of a criticism of the male prejudice which Indian politicians share with all other politicians) to say that she would certainly not have been chosen if her father had not been the great leader in the struggle for independence, Jawaharlal Nehru. Golda Meir, who became Prime Minister of Israel in 1969, seems to have been the first woman to become head of a government without any help from family connections.

It might be asked what women got from the struggle. Social and political advances are not directly related to the vote; political advance has been strictly limited almost everywhere to the right to choose between a couple of men. It is not just a joke at the women's expense to say that the important thing was that they managed to get their own way. The vote was the great issue on which men wanted to resist women – not all men, just as not all women wanted the vote. But enough men resisted to make it a real test case, and eventually the women proved their point: if there was something they really wanted, and really believed would make them equal with men, they could get it if they worked hard enough.

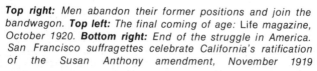

Top right: Men abandon their former positions and join the bandwagon. *Top left:* The final coming of age: Life magazine, October 1920. *Bottom right:* End of the struggle in America. San Francisco suffragettes celebrate California's ratification of the Susan Anthony amendment, November 1919

Chronology of Events

1784 The Duchess of Devonshire canvasses for Charles James Fox
at the Westminster election

1825 William Thompson's *Appeal of One Half the Human Race against
the Pretensions of the Other Half* advocates votes for women

1848 **July:** a women's rights meeting is held at Seneca Falls in
New York State

1866 **7th June:** John Stuart Mill presents his Women Suffrage
Petition to the House of Commons

1867 The Second Reform Bill is debated and Mill moves an amendment
to give votes to women. It is defeated by 194 votes to 73

1868 The National Society for Women's Suffrage is founded in England

1869 In France Léon Richier publishes *The Rights of Women*. In England, Mill's *On the Subjection of Women* is published

1871 Josephine Butler's fight against the Contagious Diseases Acts
causes dissension among the women's suffrage societies

1882 The Married Women's Property Act is passed granting married
women rights of separate ownership over every kind of property

1890 The National American Woman Suffrage Association is founded.
Wyoming becomes a state of the Union and women are given the
right to vote for Congressmen and President. During the 1890s
Western Australia, South Australia, and three more western
states in the USA enfranchise women

1893 The reforming Liberal-Labour government in New Zealand gives
women the vote

1903 **October:** the Women's Social and Political Union is founded
by Mrs Emmeline Pankhurst

1905 **13th October:** Sir Edward Grey addresses a liberal meeting in
Manchester; Annie Kenney and Christabel Pankhurst are imprisoned
for causing an uproar

1907 Finnish women are given the vote. In England suffragists and
suffragettes hold separate marches

1908 **June:** suffrage societies hold a combined procession from the
Embankment to the Albert Hall; the next weekend the WSPU
holds its own open-air demonstration at Hyde Park. Emmeline and
Christabel Pankhurst and Mrs Flora Drummond are imprisoned
after a meeting held in Trafalgar Square

1910-12 Six more American states give women the vote by
referendum

1911 In New York the Triangle Fire arouses interest in many
reforms including women's suffrage

1912 In New York suffragists parade. In England, suffragettes
heckle Lloyd George at a meeting at the Royal Albert Hall

1913 In the USA Alice Paul and Lucy Burns launch the Congressional
Union which becomes the American equivalent of the WSPU
March: a women's parade in Washington on President Wilson's
inauguration leads to a riot when it is held up by an anti-
suffrage mob
June: Emily Davison is killed when she throws herself under
King George V's horse at the Derby

1915 Denmark (including Iceland) gives women the vote

1917 Women of the Netherlands and Russia get the vote

1918 In England the Representation of the People Act gives the vote to
all men over twenty-one and all women over thirty

1920 Women get the vote in the United States

1922 All women in English-speaking Canada are enfranchised

1923 By this year Austria, Hungary, Czechoslovakia, Poland, Latvia,
Lithuania, and Esthonia have given women the vote

1928 Women in England are given the vote at twenty-one

*Top: 'Scare me, will you?': short shrift for the mouse of Man's
Supremacy **(left)**; pin-up power **(middle)**; 'The Right Dishonour-
able Double-Face Asquith' **(right)**. Centre: Keir Hardie with
suffragettes **(left)**; Rosa Luxemburg **(middle)**; Lloyd George
'land girls' **(right)**. Bottom: 'At Last!'—Punch cartoon, 1918
(left); Marie Stopes **(middle)**; 'les Tommettes' (female Tommies),
nickname of the British Women's Army Auxiliary Corps **(right)***

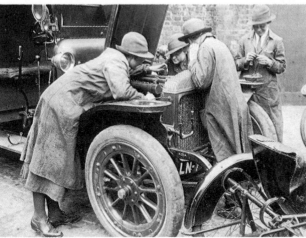

Index of main people, places and events

Author's suggestions for further reading

Some women's suffrage organisations produced massive histories of their work when the struggle was over; the American history is especially ponderous. However, *Woman Suffrage and Politics* by Carrie Chapman Catt and Nettie Shuler (Charles Scribner's and Sons, New York 1923) explains cross-currents much better than authors writing about other countries have done. Mildred Adams's *The Right of the People* (Lippincott, Philadelphia 1967) is a straightforward pro-suffrage history of the movement in the United States. Johanna Johnston's *Mrs Satan* (Macmillan, London 1968) is a sympathetic biography of Victoria Woodhull; Alice Blackwell's *Lucy Stone* (Little, Brown and Co., Boston 1930) may balance the picture by giving an account of a more orthodox early suffrage leader.

In England the respectable wing of the movement can be studied in Rachel Strachey's *Millicent Garrett Fawcett* (John Murray, London 1931) and *The Cause* (Kennikat, New York 1969) and the violent wing in Sylvia Pankhurst's *The Suffragette Movement* (Longmans, London 1931); both authors make an effort to see the case for the other wing (which is more than can be said for some Pankhurst books). Among more recent works two books by David Mitchell, *The Fighting Pankhursts* (Cape, London 1967) and *Women on the Warpath* (Cape 1966), give a good overall picture of the movement. Roger Fulford's *Votes for Women* (Faber 1957) tends to be facetious; Constance Rover's *Women's Suffrage and Party Politics 1866-1914* (Routledge, London 1967) is firmly partisan and ignores most of the difficulties of politics.

The subject attracts perhaps less attention outside the English-speaking world but Simone de Beauvoir's *The Second Sex* (Four Square Books 1969), one of the most famous feminist books of this century, has chapters about votes for women. Maurice Duverger's *Political Role of Women* (UNESCO, Paris 1955) surveys the way women have used the vote in various countries. A United Nations booklet, *Civic and Political Education of Women* (1964), gives the main dates of the struggle for every country in the world.

Library of the 20th Century will include the following titles:

Russia in Revolt
David Floyd
The Second Reich
Harold Kurtz
The Anarchists
Roderick Kedward
Suffragettes International
Trevor Lloyd
War by Time-Table
A.J.P.Taylor
Death of a Generation
Alistair Horne
Suicide of the Empires
Alan Clark
Twilight of the Habsburgs
Z.A.B.Zeman
Early Aviation
Sir Robert Saundby
Birth of the Movies
D.J.Wenden
Theodore Roosevelt
A.E.Campbell
Lenin's Russia
G.Katkov
The Weimar Republic
Sefton Delmer
Out of the Lion's Paw
Constantine Fitzgibbon
Japan: The Years of Triumph
Louis Allen
Communism Takes China
C.P.Fitzgerald
Black and White in South Africa
G.H.Le May
Woodrow Wilson
R.H.Ferrell
France 1918-34
W.Knapp
France 1934-40
A.N.Wahl
Mussolini's Italy
Geoffrey Warner
The Little Dictators
A.Polonsky
Viva Zapata
L.Bethell
The World Depression
Malcolm Falkus
Stalin's Russia
A.Nova
The Brutal Reich
Donald Watt
The Spanish Civil War
Raymond Carr
Munich: Czech Tragedy
K.G.Robbins

Trevor Lloyd was born in London in 1934 and educated at Harrow and Merton College, Oxford. He is at present Associate Professor of History at the University of Toronto. He has published *The General Election of 1880, Canada in World Affairs 1957-59*, and *Empire to Welfare State*, a history of England in the 20th century.

JM Roberts, General Editor of the *Macdonald Library of the 20th Century*, is Fellow and Tutor in Modern History at Merton College, Oxford. He is also General Editor of Purnell's *History of the 20th Century* and Joint-Editor of the *English Historical Review*, and author of *Europe 1880-1945* in the Longman's History of Europe. He has been English Editor of the *Larousse Encyclopedia of Modern History*, has reviewed for *The Observer, New Statesman,* and *Spectator,* and given talks on the BBC.

Library of the 20th Century

Publisher: Iain Sproat
Editor: Jonathan Martin
Executive Editor: Richard Johnson
Assistant Editor: Jenny Ashby
Designed by: Brian Mayers/ Germano Facetti
Research: Germano Facetti/ Gunn Brinson

Pictures selected from the following sources:

Bath Academy of Art 71 81
Bertarelli 22
Brown Brothers 41 72 79 121
Caligari 35
Central Press 95
Communist Party (UK) 4 10 65
Crown Copyright 25
Culver Pictures 48 58 76 80 123
Dazy 50 65 92
Editions Rencontre 52
Fawcett Society 37 71 84 88 89 97 122
Guaita 1 10 23 26 100 110
L. Hine 33
Imperial War Museum 98 103 109
Le Rire 16 28 86
Library of Congress 20 24 34 38 41 74 75 79 80 86 120 121 122
London Museum 56 57 61 116 123
MalMaison (Versailles) 10
Mansell Collection 10 21 22 30 44 55 114 122 123
Musée de Saint-Denis 15
Museo de Milano 103
Museum Toulouse-Lautrec-Albi 8
Novosti 123
Odhams 92 93
Press Association 63
Radio Times Hulton 24 25 36 82 123
Raphael Tuck 112
Simplicissimus 128
Snark International 7 8 11 12 16 19 21 31 35 42 47 57 106
Sport and General 88
Syndication International 91
Ullstein 36 110 111
Victoria and Albert Museum 96
Viollet 6 113
Wallace Collection 11
Wohfeld 112